BIBLE MORALS for CHILDREN

A Parent's Guide

Paul D. White
Valerie White

A Read-Together Book

BIBLE MORALS FOR CHILDREN

Copyright 2021-2023 Paul White and Valerie White.

All rights reserved. No part of this publication may be reproduced, distributed, or transmitted in any form or by any means, including photocopying, recording, or other electronic or mechanical methods, without the prior written permission of the authors. For permission requests, contact author.

All Scripture quotations are taken from the *The Holy Bible, King James Version*, except as noted. Scripture quotations marked MSG are taken from *THE MESSAGE*, copyright 1993, 2002, 2018 by Eugene H. Peterson. Used per NavPress' Fair Use Guidelines.

Bible Morals for Children: A Parent's Guide, A Read-Together Book

Originally published and printed in the United States of America

ISBN 978-1-938814-46-4

Email ordering information to **BibleMoralsForChildren@gmail.com**

Website: **BibleMoralsForChildren.com**

*Now therefore, our God, we thank thee,
and praise thy glorious name.
(The Bible, King James Version, I Chronicles 29:13)*

*To our Greatest Teacher, Christ Jesus,
and to all the wonderful Sunday School teachers
who bring the Bible's words and messages to life.*

Table of Contents

INTRODUCTION

CHAPTER 1
IN THE BEGINNING
Adam and Eve and the Garden of Eden 5
The Birth of Jesus Christ — Merry Christmas! 9

CHAPTER 2
THE RULES OF LIFE
The Ten Commandments, Not the Ten Suggestions 13
The Two Most Important Laws: Love God and Love Your Neighbor 17
The Beatitudes: Attitudes You Want to Be 21

CHAPTER 3
TRUST IN GOD FOR EVERYTHING
Abraham and Isaac — Sacrificing Your Own Son? 23
Noah's Ark — Building a Boat in the Desert 27
Gideon's 300 Soldiers Defeat an Army of 135,000 31

CHAPTER 4
MORAL COURAGE, IT'S EVERYTHING
David and Goliath — A Boy Defeats a Giant 35
Daniel, Lions', and Risking Your Life to Pray 39
Three Men and the Fiery Furnace — "But if not ..." 43

Chapter 5
FORGIVENESS
Joseph and His Brothers — Forgiving Those Who Try to Kill You 47
Cheating Your Brother, Running for Your Life 51
The Prodigal Son — You Can Go Home Again 55
The Crucifixion: What Did Jesus Say? 59

Chapter 6
OVERCOMING FEAR
Two Psalms (Songs) to Make You Feel Safe 61
Fear's Antidote 62
Losing Fear: Walking on Water 65

Chapter 7
LOOKING FOR THE PROMISED LAND
Parting of the Red Sea 67
40 Years to Walk 250 Miles 71

Chapter 8
BE GOOD AND OBEY GOD ... OR ELSE!
Jonah Swallowed by a Huge Fish 75
The Destruction of Sodom and Gomorrah 79
David and Bathsheba — Everything Wasn't Enough 83

Chapter 9
HOW DO YOU PRAY?
The Lord's Prayer 85

Chapter 10
JESUS
Overcoming the Biggest Temptations 89

Chapter 11
WANT TO BE HAPPY AND HAVE EVERYTHING?
Forget Yourself 93
Put God First! 95
Think On These Things! 97

Chapter 12
THE MATTHEW PRINCIPLE
Solving Problems with Others 99

Chapter 13
CAN GOD HEAL EVERYTHING?
Healing Mental Illness — A Man and a Herd of Pigs 103
Healing Blindness — What Did Spit Have to Do with It? 107
Healing Naaman's Leprosy and Pride 109

Chapter 14
YOU'RE SAFE ... IF YOU DON'T RUN AWAY
Put on the Whole Armor of God 113

Chapter 15
IS IT LOVE? TAKE THE TEST
What Does Real Love Look Like? The Love Chapter 117
An Example of True Love — The Story of Ruth 121

Chapter 16
HOW TO DEAL WITH SERIOUSLY BAD DAYS
The Story of Job 123

Chapter 17
NEVER, NEVER, EVER GIVE UP!
The Parable of Persistence 127
Nehemiah Building the Wall 129

Chapter 18
STOP WORRYING, YOU HAVE ENOUGH
Jesus Feeds Bread and Fish to Thousands 133
Birds and Flowers Always Have Enough and You Do Too! 137
Take Care of Others First — God's Unlimited Blessings 139
You Owe Money? Jesus Says It's Time to Go Fishing 143

Chapter 19
HAVING GREAT WISDOM
Solomon's Wish and the Best Advice Ever Given 145
Solomon's Wisdom: Whose Baby Is It? 149

Chapter 20
HEAVEN
Where Is It? What Is It Like? 153

Chapter 21
MONEY
Be Careful Not to Fall in Love! 157

Chapter 22
BEING SMART
Does Being Smart Have Anything to Do with God? 161

Chapter 23
FROM WORST TO BEST IN 3 DAYS
Paul 165

Chapter 24
DOES NUTRITION MATTER?
No! 169

Chapter 25
LOOK AGAIN!
Moses and the Burning Bush 173
Elisha and the Chariots of Fire 177

Chapter 26
   THE BIBLE AND RACE
   What Color Is God's Skin?.................................181

Chapter 27
   DEATH ... AND LIFE RESTORED!
   "It IS well" — The Shunammite's Son 185
   Dead or "Just Sleeping?" — Lazarus, Jairus' Daughter.........189

Chapter 28
   ANSWERING GOD'S CALL
   "Samuel!"...193

Chapter 29
   HOW DOES GOD JUDGE OUR LIVES?
   Judgment Day 197

Chapter 30
   THE MOST WONDERFUL STORY EVER TOLD
   Jesus Christ Rose from the Dead 201

Chapter 31
   AN EARLY PREDICTION FOR WORLD PEACE
   A Prophecy 205

CHAPTER 32
   THE WORLD'S END AND A NEW BEGINNING
   The Book of Revelation 209
   EPILOGUE

INTRODUCTION

Why would anyone want to learn about the Bible?
The Bible contains 783,137 words that have changed the world! Translated wholly or partially into over 3,300 languages, the Bible is the best-selling book of all time: over 5 billion copies, with 100 million more copies sold every year.

What are the smallest and biggest copies of the Bible ever printed?
Smallest: Etched on a silicon microchip that could fit on the head of a pin.
Biggest: 8 feet wide, 3.5 feet tall, and weighed over 1,000 pounds.

What does the word Bible mean?
It means "the books," and that's what it is: a collection of 66 books, divided into a New and Old Testament.

The first words of the Bible were written over 3,000 years ago, and the rest of the Bible took over 1,000 years to complete. It was written by about 40 different authors living on three different continents in a combination of three different languages: Hebrew, Greek, and Aramaic.

How was the entire Bible put together?
People would tell stories about God and what they learned about him. This information was passed down from generation to generation. Eventually, many of the teachings were written down and collected into one book.

What is the Bible about?
It is the story of mankind learning about the One God and turning to him to find salvation, to be saved from bad and wrong things, so they can live happily forever.

The Bible includes:

- Rules to be obeyed and customs to follow.
- Stories of people who overcame every imaginable problem by faith, moral courage, and obedience to God.
- Some of the best known songs, prayers, laws, and wise words ever written.

BIBLE MORALS FOR CHILDREN

How does the Bible begin and end?

It begins with God choosing a special people, the Hebrews or Israelites, to lead the rest of the world to worship him. Starting with the first division of the Bible, usually referred to as the Old Testament, God said he would send a savior, a messiah who would save the world. Christians believe that the Messiah was and is Jesus Christ. Jews believe that the Messiah has not yet come.

The other main section of the Bible, known as the New Testament, starts with the birth of Jesus Christ. It tells about his life and the lives of his followers. The New Testament ends with the Book of Revelation which describes the future of the world and the great and final battle between Good and evil.

Is the Bible true?
- Christians believe the entire Bible is the true Word of God.
- Jews believe that the Old Testament alone is the true Word of God.
- Atheists don't believe in God, but still accept many Bible stories as providing positive lessons on behavior and character.

For centuries, *billions* of people have agreed that the Bible is the most proven source for helping anyone of any age to learn about morals and values. It teaches how to live our lives in a way that brings love, peace, health, happiness, wisdom, protection, direction, and abundance.

What is the purpose of this book?
It provides a high-interest moral perspective on the Bible's most well-known teachings and stories. It does not attempt to teach the entire Bible. Nothing can substitute for studying the Bible itself in its entirety.

Why did we write this book?
To interest readers in learning more about the Bible and to encourage them to build their lives on a spiritually moral foundation that is stronger than any problems they will ever face.

"And all thy children shall be taught of the LORD; and great shall be the peace of thy children."
(Isaiah 54:13)

BIBLE MORALS FOR CHILDREN

"And the LORD God planted a garden eastward in Eden; and there he put the man whom he had formed."
(Genesis 2:8)

CHAPTER 1

IN THE BEGINNING

ADAM AND EVE AND THE GARDEN OF EDEN

Genesis: 1–3

The Bible book of Genesis tells how God created the world and the first people, Adam and Eve. Were they created from dust and a rib as the story says? Is the Adam and Eve story an allegory, a story with hidden meaning, to teach people about the need to obey God?

We can all agree on the main principles of the story. God gave Adam and Eve a perfect place to live, the Garden of Eden, where they had everything they needed. God told Adam and Eve that they could use and enjoy everything in the Garden of Eden with one exception: they should not touch the Tree of the Knowledge of Good and Evil because it would destroy them. Was God talking about a tree with poisonous fruit, or was God warning Adam and Eve to avoid the temptation to mix good things with a small amount of evil in their lives? Was it a warning to them and us to obey God, rather than deciding for ourselves what is right and wrong?

What did Adam and Eve do? The Bible says the fruit of the tree looked and tasted good. In our lives, a little bit of the wrong thing can often look harmless and fun. As Eve was deciding what to do, a talking snake approached her. It told Eve that if she and Adam ate of that fruit and disobeyed God, "Ye shall not surely die:" (Genesis 3:4). It said God didn't want Adam and Eve to eat the forbidden fruit because God knew it would make them smart and able to decide between right and wrong for themselves. Adam and Eve would then be like gods and wouldn't need the real God any longer.

The snake's tricky argument convinced Eve. She ate the fruit, and she talked Adam into eating it. When God showed up in the Garden of Eden to visit them, they felt so guilty, they hid. That's when God knew they had disobeyed him.

The Bible says God proceeded to kick Adam and Eve out of the Garden of Eden.

He told them that from that day forward, many activities in their lives were going to be *much* more difficult for them and all their future children.

We all have opportunities to turn our lives into Gardens of Eden with a good education, good jobs, peaceful homes, health, safety, and good friends. We simply need to follow what the Bible teaches. It tells us to respect our parents, tell the truth, work hard in school or at your job, obey the law, treat everyone with respect, be forgiving and unselfish, and so forth. When we practice these traits in our lives, we stay in our Garden of Eden. When we try to mix right and wrong, we risk losing the blessings that make our lives a true paradise.

Something to Think About

Even though God gave Adam and Eve everything they needed in the Garden of Eden, it wasn't enough for them. They disobeyed God in the one thing he commanded them not to do, and lost everything.

- Which of your parents' rules are you most tempted to break: Why?
- Why do you think that rule is important to your parents?

*"And God saw every thing that he had made,
and, behold, it was very good."
(Genesis 1:31)*

BIBLE MORALS FOR CHILDREN

"And they came with haste, and found Mary, and Joseph, and the babe lying in a manger."
(Luke 2:16)

IN THE BEGINNING

THE BIRTH OF JESUS CHRIST — MERRY CHRISTMAS!

Matthew: 1, Luke: 2

The birth of Jesus of Nazareth was unique in many ways. *Christ* wasn't his last name, but a title given to him later in life. His birth and life experiences were predicted over fifty times in the Bible, hundreds of years before his birth. The Jews were waiting for the Messiah, the Savior who would be a warrior king, save them from persecution, and lead them to a wonderful future. The Jews eventually decided that Jesus wasn't the savior they were waiting for, while Christians believe that Jesus' birth fulfilled the prophecy of the Messiah coming to earth.

The Bible says Jesus was born to a virgin mother, Mary. That means that God was Jesus' father, not Joseph. Mary became pregnant before she and Joseph were married, and Joseph agreed to accept the baby. He must have had an incredibly strong faith in God! An angel from God gave Joseph this message: "Joseph, thou son of David, fear not to take unto thee Mary thy wife: for that which is conceived in her is of the Holy Ghost" (Matthew 1:20).

All the symbols we associate with Christmas result from the details of Jesus' birth. He was born in a barn in the city of Bethlehem because it was a busy time of year, and none of the local hotels had any room. Baby Jesus' bed was a manger, a trough used to hold hay for farm animals. Wise Men from another country were led by a special star in the sky to travel to the barn and bring valuable gifts. They had been told by God that a new king was being born. Local shepherds out in their fields were told by singing angels to go to the barn and honor this newborn future king, and they did. It would have been pretty crowded in that small barn on that special night, and quite a sight for a new baby!

Celebrating Christmas has a religious origin, the birth of Jesus. *Christmas* means celebration of the Christ or Savior. Today, Christmas is celebrated on December 25, but historical records show that Jesus' actual birth date could have been December, September, or even March. No one knows for sure, but no one feels the exact date matters much in terms of celebrating this wonderful event. What about the traditional Christmas celebrations with Santa Claus, Christmas trees, gift giving, and parties with friends and family? All of these practices were developed as people in many countries heard about Christmas. They created fun social activities that reminded them of different parts of the original Christmas story.

The social activities of Christmas have gotten so popular today that people often lose sight of the real Christmas story. When we hear people say they want to celebrate the *real* meaning of Christmas, they're referring to their desire to not focus on food, parties, and gift giving. Instead, they want to quietly remember the important lessons from that dark night when Jesus was born, centuries ago. God called a group of ordinary people to an old barn filled with farm animals to celebrate the birth of the most special baby ever born. Celebrating the real meaning of Christmas means filling our lives with the ideas from God that were present that night: purity, trust, obedience to God, fearlessness, unselfishness, humility, and love for others.

Something to Think About
• Why did God choose Jesus, the greatest man who ever lived, to be born in a barn with farm animals and ordinary people?
• Do you celebrate Christmas with more of the religious meaning or the secular meaning?
• Would you like to change anything about how you celebrate this special holiday?

"For unto you is born this day in the city of David a Saviour, which is Christ the Lord."
(Luke 2:11)

BIBLE MORALS FOR CHILDREN

"And the LORD said unto Moses, Come up to me into the mount, and be there: and I will give thee tables of stone, and a law, and commandments which I have written; that thou mayest teach them."
(Exodus 24:12)

CHAPTER 2

THE RULES OF LIFE

THE TEN COMMANDMENTS, NOT THE TEN SUGGESTIONS

Exodus: 20

The Ten Commandments have been described as *protective fences around bottomless pits*. Accepted by both Jews and Christians, these commandments are God's rules for how we should worship him and behave morally toward each other. They are also known as the *Decalogue*.

God convinced the Egyptian slave holders to release the Hebrews with Moses as their leader. Many gods were worshipped in Egypt, but the Hebrews began worshipping the One God. For forty years, Moses led them through the wilderness searching for the Promised Land that God had said waiting for them. Eventually, the Hebrews sarrived at a large mountain named Mount Sinai. God told Moses to go to the top of this mountain to receive the ten most important laws for the Hebrews to follow. Moses was on Mount Sinai with God for forty days. When he came down from the mountain, he had two stone tablets that God had given him with the Ten Commandments carved on them. Here is the list.

FIRST: There is only One God, and he is the only god we are to worship. Coming from Egypt where they worshipped over 2,000 gods, this was a real change for the Hebrews. God said we should turn only to him for our every need. "I am the LORD thy God, which have brought thee out of the land of Egypt, out of the house of bondage. Thou shalt have no other gods before me" (Exodus 20:2–3).

SECOND: This One God is Spirit, so we should not worship any idols or material objects. That includes not making a god or idol out of material things, like money, human importance, physical appearance, or even other people.

THIRD: Do not take God's name in vain. We often hear people use the name of

God or Jesus as if it were a casual word or even a swear word. God says we are *never* to do that. The Ten Commandments teach that we are to use the name of God only in a respectful, holy way.

FOURTH: Remember the Sabbath day to keep it holy. The sabbath, or holy day, varies according to religions and denominations. For Jews, the Sabbath is Saturday. For most Christian denominations it's Sunday, while Friday is the holy day for Muslims. Is there just *one* day in the week that God wants us to be good and obey him? Aren't *all* of the days holy to God? Imagine what the world could be like if people honored and obeyed God *every* day, and didn't limit it to Friday, Saturday, or Sunday?

FIFTH: Honor your father and mother. God chose an interesting word with *honor*. It means to *respect* or do what we've promised. This Commandment doesn't say we must always *agree* with our parents, or *like* what they're telling us to do. It says we always need to be respectful and keep our word when we've told our parents that we will or won't do something. When children honor their parents in this way, it creates a wonderful, long-lasting relationship that blesses everyone.

SIXTH: Don't kill. Life is from God. It's indescribably precious. This commandment tells us to have respect for the great gift of life that God has given us and to protect and care for every living thing.

SEVENTH: Don't commit adultery. This commandment says that once we're married, we keep ourselves for our husband or wife, and no one else. This includes what we do and what we think about doing. There's even a bigger meaning to this commandment that applies to everyone whether they're married or not. To adulterate something is to make it impure. This commandment includes keeping all of our thoughts, words, and deeds pure, kind, unselfish, and honest with everyone.

EIGHTH: Don't Steal. If something doesn't belong to us, no matter how big or small, we never take it. No excuses. No exceptions.

NINTH: Don't Lie. How important are truth and honesty? Without them, our world would collapse. Without truth and honesty in our lives, *we* collapse.

TENTH: Don't Covet. Coveting is yearning for something we don't have. It makes us jealous, dissatisfied, and ungrateful for what we do have. The way to avoid coveting is to stay grateful for what God has given us.

Something to Think About
- The Ten Commandments lists respecting your parents and not lying, as equally important as not killing. Why?
- Which Commandments do you break the most?
- Do you think any other commandments should have been added to the original ten?

BIBLE MORALS FOR CHILDREN

"And Jesus answering said, A certain man went down from Jerusalem to Jericho, and fell among thieves, which stripped him of his raiment, and wounded him, and departed, leaving him half dead" (Luke 10:30).

THE RULES OF LIFE

THE TWO MOST IMPORTANT LAWS: LOVE GOD AND LOVE YOUR NEIGHBOR

Luke: 10; Matthew 22

One time when Jesus was talking to a crowd, a lawyer asked him a question. He asked Jesus which law of God was the *most* important one that a person should follow. This was tricky because at that time, the Jews had over 600 laws in the Torah, the books of the Bible that they studied. Jesus answered that the most important law was to love God with all your heart, mind, soul, and strength. Then he added that there was a second part that was also important, "Thou shalt love thy neighbour as thyself" (Matthew 22:39). Wanting a more detailed explanation, the lawyer asked, "And who is my neighbour?" (Luke 10:29). Jesus answered the question by telling a parable, an earthly story with a heavenly message. It's become known as the "Story of the Good Samaritan."

The story says a Jewish man was walking between the towns of Jerusalem and Jericho. He was robbed and brutally beaten by a group of thieves and then left by the side of the road.

First, a Jewish priest walked by and saw the injured man. The priest crossed to the other side of the road, kept walking, and did nothing to help the man.

Later, a man from a similar religious group walked by and saw the injured man, but also did nothing to help him.

The third man to come along was a Samaritan, a group of people who hated the Jews and vice-versa, but he immediately stopped to help the Jewish man. He cleaned up the man's wounds, put him on his donkey, and took him to a local hotel. The Samaritan rented a room for the man and paid for it himself. He stayed with the man overnight, nursing and caring for him. The next morning, the Samaritan left extra money with the hotel manager, so the injured man could stay at the hotel until he was able to take care of himself.

Jesus said that this kind of caring for our fellow man is what it means to love and obey God. We show our love for God, not by what we say, but by how we express our love for all mankind. The Samaritan sacrificed his time, money, and safety to help a man he didn't even know. To this day, someone who does an unselfish good deed for a needy stranger is often referred to as a *good samaritan*.

BIBLE MORALS FOR CHILDREN

Something to Think About

- The Good Samaritan risked his own safety and sacrificed his time and money to help an enemy. What part of the Good Samaritan's unselfish actions would have been the most difficult for you to do?

"Jesus said unto him, Thou shalt love the Lord thy God with all thy heart, and with all thy soul, and with all thy mind. This is the first and great commandment. And the second is like unto it, Thou shalt love they neighbour as thyself."
(Matthew 22:37–39)

BIBLE MORALS FOR CHILDREN

"And he opened his mouth and taught them, saying, Blessed are the poor in spirit: for theirs is the kingdom of heaven." (Matthew 5:2–3)

THE RULES OF LIFE

THE BEATITUDES: ATTITUDES YOU WANT TO BE

Matthew: 5

One of Jesus' most important talks is called the *Sermon on the Mount*. In this talk, he included a list of behaviors or attitudes called *beatitudes* that can make a person's life wonderful beyond description. The beatitude means *blessed*. Jesus said we will be blessed:

- If we are humble and not conceited about ourselves and our accomplishments.
- If we have faith and trust in God when sad or challenged with problems.
- If we are unselfish and patient with others.
- If we are unafraid to take a strong public stand for what is morally good.
- If we are forgiving of others, just as we want others to be toward us.
- If we are pure in our thoughts, words, and deeds.
- If we have the moral courage to be a peace maker. Being a peace lover is much easier, but it doesn't accomplish much.
- If we are willing to sacrifice our reputation or safety to do what is morally right toward others or for God.

Jesus said it wasn't enough to just know the beatitudes. We have to live them. "If ye know these things, happy are ye if ye do them" (John 13:17). We usually don't think it's a blessing when we have to give up things that we like, or when we get attacked for doing what's right. Jesus said that if we make doing the right thing the top priority in our lives, we can trust God to show us how those experiences will bless us.

Something to Think About
- Think of a time you tried to be a peace-maker. How did it turn out?
- Why is being a peace *maker* more difficult than being a peace *lover*?

BIBLE MORALS FOR CHILDREN

"And he [God] said, Take now thy son, thine only son Isaac, whom thou lovest, and get thee into the land of Moriah; and offer him there for a burnt offering ...."
(Genesis 22:2)

CHAPTER 3

TRUST IN GOD FOR EVERYTHING

ABRAHAM AND ISAAC — SACRIFICING YOUR OWN SON?

Genesis: 22

Abraham was one of God's special prophets. God called him to go to a strange, new land and become the father of a new nation. Abraham obeyed because he had an unshakable faith in God. Years later, God promised Abraham a son with his wife, Sarah, even though she was 90 years old and Abraham was 100. Sarah did give birth to a baby they named Isaac.

Isaac, Abraham's only son with Sarah, was precious to him, but God wanted to be sure that Abraham put obedience to God above *everything* else. He decided to test Abraham's faith without him knowing about it. God told Abraham to take Isaac up to a mountain and sacrifice him on an altar. Abraham didn't panic, beg, or refuse to follow God's command. He just told the young Isaac to load up their donkey with firewood because they were going up the mountain to make a sacrifice to God. At that time in history, Abraham and all Hebrews made animal sacrifices to God.

When Abraham and Isaac got to the mountain, Abraham started placing firewood on an altar. Isaac saw no animal to sacrifice and said to his father, "My father: ... Behold the fire and the wood: but where is the lamb for a burnt offering? And Abraham said, My son, God will provide himself a lamb for a burnt offering: ..." (Genesis 22: 7–8).

Abraham proceeded to lay Isaac down on the firewood and tie him up with the rope. He then reached for his knife to kill his son! It's impossible to imagine what Abraham and Isaac's thoughts must have been at that moment!

At the moment when Abraham was ready to sacrifice his own son, an angel from heaven called out to him and said *not* to harm Isaac. The angel said that there was no need to take Isaac's life because Abraham had shown God how much faith he had in him, even to the point of being willing to sacrifice the son he deeply loved. Abraham then heard a noise. It was a sheep stuck in the nearby bushes. Abraham was able to catch it and use it for the sacrifice instead of his son.

God now trusted Abraham completely. He went on to be considered the father of both the Jewish and Christian religions.

The gripping story of Abraham and Isaac is one of many Bible stories that teach how a strong commitment to moral and spiritual values and an unwavering trust in God bring us the protection and blessings that God promises us.

Something to Think About:
- Would you have been able to trust God as much as Abraham did?
- What request from God would be the most difficult for you to do?

"Trust in the LORD with all thine heart; and lean not unto thine own understanding. In all thy ways acknowledge him, and he shall direct thy paths."
(Proverbs 3:5, 6)

BIBLE MORALS FOR CHILDREN

"[And God said unto Noah,] Make thee an ark ..."
(Genesis 6:14).
"And of every living thing of all flesh, two of every sort shalt
thou bring into the ark, ..."
(Genesis 6:19)

TRUST IN GOD FOR EVERYTHING

NOAH'S ARK — BUILDING A BOAT IN THE DESERT

Genesis: 6–9

The story of Noah and the Ark is known to most people, but what makes it useful in our lives are some of the details.

The world's people were acting wickedly toward each other. God decided to destroy them all and start over except for Noah and his family because the Bible says they "found grace in the eyes of the LORD" (Genesis 6:8). God told Noah to build a huge ark, a covered boat, and put his entire family inside it along with a male and female pair of every living thing. God said he would then make it rain for forty days which would flood the entire earth and destroy all other life. Once the rain stopped and all the wicked people were dead, Noah, his family, and the animals could leave the ark to start re-populating the earth. The Bible says that's what they did.

Here are a few more story details that helped Noah live a better life, and can help us do the same thing.

- Noah was over 500 years old when God told him to build the ark, so Noah had much work to do. He didn't complain that he was too old to work.
- It possibly took more than 100 years for Noah to build the ark, so he was a person who didn't give up easily.
- God told Noah to build the ark in a desert area where there were no large bodies of water. Noah must have had complete faith in God's Word. He wasn't discouraged by the many friends and neighbors who probably criticized or made fun of him.
- Noah was cooped up in the ark for 40 days with his family members and many smelly animals. He must have had a lot of patience and the ability to get along with others when there were disagreements.

The final detail of the story is a happy one. The rain finally stopped, the flood waters dried up, and Noah, his family, and the animals were able to come out of the ark to start rebuilding the earth. With all life now gone except for Noah, his family, and the animals, they were likely afraid that God would cause another flood if he were to be angry again. To help Noah's family not be fearful, God told them that every time it rained in the future, he would also put a rainbow in the sky. It would symbolize God's love for his creation and a promise that he would never destroy the earth again. "I do set my bow in the cloud, and it shall be for a token of a covenant between me and the earth" (Genesis 9:13).

Something to Think About
Noah must have been mocked by his friends and family while he spent years and years building a boat in the desert. How have you dealt with people who make fun of your dreams and plans?

"For with God nothing shall be impossible."
(Luke 1:37)

"[And they] blew the trumpets, and brake the pitcher, ... and they cried, The sword of the LORD, and of Gideon."
(Judges 7:20).

TRUST IN GOD FOR EVERYTHING

GIDEON'S 300 SOLDIERS DEFEAT AN ARMY OF 135,000

Judges: 6–8

The Bible says God let an enemy tribe rule over the Israelites for seven years because God was angry at the Israelites for worshipping idols. Finally, God decided to allow the Israelites to defeat the enemy tribe. He chose a young man named Gideon to lead them.

An angel appeared to Gideon to deliver the news that he should lead the fight. Gideon didn't believe the message was from God, so he asked for proof. The angel caused some food that Gideon was holding to burst into flames. Gideon then believed the angel's message!

Next, God wanted to test Gideon to see if he would be able to lead the Israelite's army. God told him to destroy one of the idols Gideon's people were worshipping. Gideon could have been killed for doing this, but he did what God requested. God was happy Gideon obeyed him, so he began preparing Gideon to defeat the enemy tribe.

Gideon recruited 32,000 Israelites to fight against the enemy army of 135,000 soldiers! Gideon felt it would be impossible to defeat such a great number of soldiers, so he prayed to God and asked for help. God provided the help, but not in the way Gideon expected.

God told Gideon that he had *too many* soldiers! If Gideon were to defeat the enemy army, he would believe he was responsible for the victory instead of giving all credit to God. God gave Gideon several tests to reduce the size of his army. Gideon ended up with just 300 soldiers to fight against the enemy's 135,000!

If that wasn't a big enough challenge, God sent Gideon's army into battle without any weapons! God told Gideon to go into battle armed only with trumpets and jars containing burning torches. At every step, Gideon had no idea how his army would be successful, but he trusted God to lead him. Gideon followed God's plan.

Gideon's army snuck up on the enemy camp at night from several directions. At the right moment, they all charged into the camp making loud noises with the trumpets and breaking open the jars containing the flaming torches. The noise from the trumpets and breaking jars, and the bright lights from the torches caused great confusion everywhere in the camp. Gideon's soldiers also continued yelling loudly during their attack, "The sword of the LORD, and of Gideon" (Judges 7:20). All of this was too much for the enemy army, and they ran away in panic!

Gideon next sent messages to the rest of the Israelites telling them to capture the enemy soldiers who were running away. In the end, Gideon's soldiers were safe, the enemy's army was defeated, and Israel regained its freedom.

The story of Gideon reminds us that no matter how incapable we feel, and no matter how impossible a situation might look, anything good is possible if we are willing to trust and obey God.

Something to Think About
- Have you ever been outnumbered when you were trying to accomplish something?
- How did you handle the situation?

"Fear not: for they that be with us are more than they that be with them."
(II Kings 6:16)

BIBLE MORALS FOR CHILDREN

"And it came to pass, when [Goliath] the Philistine arose,
and came and drew nigh to meet David, that David hasted,
and ran toward the army to meet the Philistine."
(I Samuel 17:48)

CHAPTER 4

MORAL COURAGE, IT'S EVERYTHING

DAVID AND GOLIATH — A BOY DEFEATS A GIANT

I Samuel: 17

David was an Israelite shepherd, and the youngest of his dad's eight sons. He was a teenager who barely stood five feet tall. Goliath, a Philistine and David's enemy, was a gigantic warrior who stood more than two feet taller than David.

The Philistines wanted to fight and defeat the Israelite army because they disagreed about their religions and who should control some nearby land. The armies of the Israelites and Philistines camped opposite each other across a valley, ready to begin their battle. One day, Goliath came out between the two armies and challenged the Israelites to send one single man to fight him. The winner of this single fight would bring victory to their entire army. Goliath repeated this challenge for 40 days because the Israelites didn't have one soldier brave enough to fight him. They believed Goliath would slaughter them. Goliath wasn't just huge, he was incredibly strong! His suit of armor weighed almost 150 pounds, and he carried a spear with a 15-pound spearhead!

David learned about the problem with Goliath when David's dad sent him to the battlefield to deliver food to his soldier brothers. While there, David heard Goliath insulting the Israelites' God. He immediately told King Saul, the head of the Israelites' army, that he would go out to meet Goliath in battle.

King Saul tried to talk David out of volunteering to fight Goliath: "Thou art not able to go against this Philistine to fight with him: for thou art but a youth, and he a man of war from his youth" (I Samuel 17:33). David explained that when he was a shepherd, he had previously fought and killed both a lion and a bear by himself. He was certain God would also provide a way for him to defeat Goliath. Saul then agreed to let David fight, but told him he needed to put on all the heavy armor and carry all of the large weapons soldiers used back then. David told Saul that he wouldn't wear or carry any of those weapons because he knew his success would come from trusting God, as it always had. All David took to the fight was a sling, a weapon similar to a slingshot, and five smooth stones as ammunition.

When Goliath saw little David coming out to fight him, he was insulted. He started trying to intimidate David with threats of how he was going to kill him. David told Goliath he wasn't afraid because Goliath was fighting for evil things while David was fighting to honor God. David was so confident in God's protection that he ran toward Goliath to fight him! When he got close enough, David put one small stone in his sling and slung it at Goliath. It hit him in the forehead in one of the few, small, exposed spots that Goliath's armor didn't cover. Goliath fell to the ground and died. The Israelite army was victorious and saved!

What a great lesson to remember when we face our own scary, giant-sized problems. Like David, we can:

- Focus on taking a stand for what's right, rather than worrying about what might happen to us if we take that stand.
- Get our confidence and courage from remembering previous times when God has saved and rescued us. No matter how big our problems seem to be, God is bigger!
- Remember to be ourselves, and to not feel pressured to act, talk, or look like anyone else.

Something to Think About
- When we face Goliath-sized problems in our own lives, sometimes we might stay and fight and other times we might run. Think of a Goliath-sized problem that has occurred in your life. Did you confront the problem and fight it, or did you avoid it? Looking back, do you think you made the right decision?

*"Not by might, nor by power, but by my spirit,
saith the LORD of hosts."
(Zechariah 4:6)*

BIBLE MORALS FOR CHILDREN

*"Then the king commanded, and they brought Daniel,
and cast him into the den of lions."
(Daniel 6:16).*

MORAL COURAGE, IT'S EVERYTHING

DANIEL, LIONS', AND RISKING YOUR LIFE TO PRAY

Daniel: 6

Daniel was the top advisor to a King named Darius who worshipped other gods, not the One God Daniel worshipped. The King's other advisors were jealous of Daniel and plotted to get rid of him. They went to King Darius and encouraged him to sign a law saying that any person who prayed to any god or man but the King would be thrown into a den of lions to be killed. The other advisors wanted this law because they knew Daniel prayed to the One God every day. They knew Daniel would continue his daily prayers no matter what. King Darius let his pride get the better of him and agreed to sign this law. Sure enough, Daniel kept praying, even after he was told about the new law. When it came time that day to worship his God, Daniel opened the window to his room, so everyone could see him pray.

The other advisors immediately went to the King to report that Daniel had broken the new law, and reminded the King that he must throw Daniel to the lions. King Darius felt terrible because he realized he'd been tricked. The King greatly valued Daniel but had no choice but to follow the law he'd signed. Daniel was thrown into the lions' den. Before the king returned to his palace for the night, he called to Daniel hoping Daniel's God would save him.

The King felt terrible about what he'd done to Daniel. He stayed up all night worrying about him. In the morning, the King hurried over to the lions' den and called to Daniel to see if he was still alive: "O Daniel, servant of the living God, is thy God, whom thou servest continually, able to deliver thee from the lions?" (Daniel 6:20). Daniel wasn't angry at the King. He replied that God had kept the lions from hurting him because Daniel had done nothing wrong to King Darius and had remained faithful to God.

The King, overjoyed that Daniel was still alive, decreed that everyone in his kingdom should now worship Daniel's God. Daniel's unshakable faith and trust in God saved his own life, but also improved the lives of everyone in the kingdom. What happened to the advisors who tricked the King and tried to get Daniel killed? The Bible says *they* were thrown into the lions' den as punishment.

Something to Think About

• A famous drawing of Daniel in the lions' den shows him looking out of a window at the sky, and ignoring the lions circling around him. What do you think the artist was saying about how Daniel chose to protect himself?

"Behold, I give unto you power to tread on serpents and scorpions, and over all the power of the enemy: and nothing shall by any means hurt you."
(Luke 10:19)

BIBLE MORALS FOR CHILDREN

"[The king] said, Did not we cast three men bound into the midst of the fire? ..." (Daniel 3:23). "Lo, I see four men loose, walking in the midst of the fire, and they have no hurt; and the form of the fourth is like the Son of God."
(Daniel 3:25)

MORAL COURAGE, IT'S EVERYTHING

THREE MEN AND THE FIERY FURNACE — "BUT IF NOT ..."

Daniel: 3

Shadrach, Meshach, and Abednego were three Hebrew men who held important jobs for Nebuchadnezzar, the King of Babylon. The King's many other employees were not Hebrews and worshipped other gods. They were jealous of Shadrach, Meshach, and Abednego and wanted to get rid of them.

One day, the other employees thought of a way to get the three Hebrews killed. King Nebuchadnezzar had a new, huge golden idol 90 feet tall and 9 feet thick. He commanded all his subjects to bow down and worship the statue at certain times every day. If anyone refused to bow down, the King said he would throw them into a large fiery furnace he used for killing people. Shadrach, Meshach, and Abednego believed in the One God more than anything, so when it came time to bow down to the golden idol, the three men refused.

Immediately, their jealous co-workers reported this to the king, and the king called for them to be brought before him. He was furious with them for not bowing down to the golden idol. King Nebuchadnezzar offered the men one final chance to bow down and save their lives. He reminded them how hot the furnace was and asked them if they thought their God could rescue them if they were thrown into the fire.

Shadrach, Meshach, and Abednego calmly told the king: "If it be so, our God whom we serve is able to deliver us from the burning fiery furnace, and he will deliver us out of thine hand, O king. But if not, be it known unto thee, O king, that we will not serve thy gods, nor worship the golden image which thou hast set up" (Daniel 3:17, 18). Whether it cost them their lives or not, the three men were not going to turn away from their God and worship idols!

The men's refusal to obey the King made him furious! He ordered his soldiers to heat up the fire seven times hotter than it had ever been heated, and all three men, fully clothed, were thrown into the furnace.

King Nebuchadnezzar looked through an opening into the fiery furnace and was amazed. He didn't see three dead men. He saw four men walking around in the furnace unharmed. The first three men were Shadrach, Meshach, and

Abednego, but the fourth man, the King said, looked like the Son of God.

Nebuchadnezzar was convinced that the three men had been saved by the One God they worshipped and ordered the men to immediately be removed from the fiery furnace. The Bible says that the men were not burned, and their clothes didn't even smell like fire! King Nebuchadnezzar was convinced that Shadrach, Meshach, and Abednego's One God was the true God. He declared that his entire kingdom would worship the One God from that day forward.

Sometimes it seems like we will lose out on good things if we don't compromise the values and principles we believe in. Giving in can be tempting. Sticking to our values and principles can seem dangerous or scary. It's likely the three Hebrew men were terrified of being thrown into the fiery furnace, but their faith and trust in God was greater than their fear. They didn't compromise their principles, and they were protected.

Something to Think About
• People are able to do some very brave things when they don't let their fear stop them from doing the right thing. What's something you felt was right to do even though you were scared to do it?

"When thou passest through the waters, I will be with thee; and through the rivers, they shall not overflow thee: when thou walkest through the fire, thou shalt not be burned; neither shall the flame kindle upon thee."
(Isaiah 43:2)

BIBLE MORALS FOR CHILDREN

"And it came to pass, when Joseph was come unto his
brethren, that they stript Joseph out of his coat,
his coat of many colours that was on him;
And they took him, and cast him into a pit: ...."
(Genesis 37:23–24)

Chapter 5

FORGIVENESS

JOSEPH AND HIS BROTHERS — FORGIVING THOSE WHO TRY TO KILL YOU

Genesis: 37–45

The Bible story of Joseph and his brothers teaches that forgiving others who treat you badly is how we avoid being harmed by our own hatred.

Joseph was the youngest of eleven brothers who were jealous of Joseph because he was their father's favorite. One night, Joseph had a dream. The dream's message told Joseph that he was better than his brothers. Joseph made the mistake of telling his brothers about his dream. Hearing the dream's message, they decided to get rid of Joseph once and for all. They came up with a plan to throw Joseph into a pit in the fields far from home where they worked. They would leave him there alone to be eaten by wild animals.

One day soon after, the brothers took Joseph's coat of many colors, a special gift given to Joseph by his father, and poured animal blood on it. Then they threw Joseph into the pit and left him. When the brothers got home, they lied to their dad, showed him the coat of many colors covered in blood, and told him that Joseph had been killed by wild animals. Even though Joseph was left in a horribly scary situation by his brothers who treated him cruelly, he didn't hate his brothers.

Soon after being left in the pit, some slave traders came along and found Joseph. They took him to Egypt where he was sold as a slave to Potiphar, an officer in Pharaoh's army. Joseph worked hard to be Potiphar's best servant. He did such a good job, he was placed in charge of Potiphar's whole house! Everything was fine until Potiphar's wife tried to force Joseph to be her boyfriend. "But he refused, and said unto his master's wife, Behold, my master wotteth not what is with me in the house, and he hath committed all that he hath to my hand; There is none greater in this house than I; neither hath he kept back any thing from me but thee, because thou art his wife: how then can I do this great wickedness, and sin against God? (Genesis 39:8–9). Potiphar's wife was angry, so she lied, saying Joseph had attacked her. Potiphar believed his wife's lie and put Joseph in Pharaoh's prison. Even so, Joseph refused to hate Potiphar and his wife.

In prison, Joseph became such a good prisoner that he was put in charge of the other prisoners. While there, he interpreted another prisoner's dream. When Pharaoh heard about Joseph's ability, Pharaoh asked him to interpret his own troubling dream. Joseph explained what the dream meant: Pharaoh must save lots of food for the next seven years. There would be a great famine in the land of Egypt, a time when food would become scarce. Pharaoh was grateful and put Joseph in charge of preparing for the famine in all of Egypt.

The famine came seven years later, but everyone in Egypt had food because of Joseph's preparation. Some lands, such as the one where Joseph's hateful brothers lived, had not prepared for the famine. They came to Egypt to beg the man in charge to sell them food. They didn't recognize the man, but it was Joseph, the brother they believed they'd killed. Joseph, however, did recognize his brothers, but said nothing about who he truly was. Joseph talked to his brothers for a while before agreeing to sell them food. He asked about their family, and they admitted the terrible thing they'd done to their youngest brother, Joseph, years before. After his brothers admitted what they'd done, Joseph agreed to give them food and told them who he was. Joseph forgave them and still felt no hate.

Joseph believed all the things that had happened to him were God's plan to keep his brothers and his dad from starving. If Joseph had not forgiven all of the terrible things others had done to him, and instead had become bitter and hateful, he never would have been able to save the entire nation of Egypt and his own family from starvation.

Something to Think About
• Joseph had every reason to hate his brothers, but he chose to forgive them. Is there anyone you have a reason to hate, but instead have chosen, or could choose to forgive?

"Then came Peter to him, and said, Lord, how oft shall my brother sin against me, and I forgive him? till seven times? Jesus saith unto him, I say not unto thee, Until seven times: but, Until seventy times seven."
(Matthew 18:21–22, King James Version)

BIBLE MORALS FOR CHILDREN

"And Esau ran to meet him [Jacob], and embraced him, and fell on his neck, and kissed him: and they wept."
(Genesis 33:4)

FORGIVENESS

CHEATING YOUR BROTHER, RUNNING FOR YOUR LIFE

Genesis: 27–33

Jacob and Esau were twin brothers. Jacob was his mother's favorite, and Esau, the oldest son, was his dad's. When their dad, Isaac, became very old, he told Esau to prepare his favorite food for him, so he could eat it and then give Esau his blessing. Receiving Isaac's blessing meant Esau would inherit most of his dad's possessions. Esau left their house and went out to hunt for the food to cook for his dad.

Meanwhile, Jacob and Esau's mother, Rebecca, heard what Isaac had said. She didn't want her favorite son, Jacob, to lose the inheritance, so she made the special food Isaac had requested. She told Jacob to take the food to Isaac quickly before Esau returned from hunting. To fool Isaac, Rebecca helped Jacob disguise himself to look like his brother Esau. This wasn't difficult because Isaac could barely see.

Jacob went to his dad, pretending to be Esau, and gave him the food. Isaac ate the food, and then gave Jacob his blessing. Finally, Esau came back from hunting and gave Isaac the food he had requested. Esau was terribly upset when Isaac told him he had already given his blessing to his brother Jacob. Therefore, Esau would receive almost no inheritance! Esau was furious with Jacob for stealing his inheritance. He swore to himself that he would kill Jacob as soon as their dad had died.

Rebekah heard Esau's promise to kill his brother, so she told Jacob he must leave their home immediately to live with his uncle. Jacob escaped from Esau, and worked for his uncle for many years. Jacob grew older and raised a family of his own, but he never saw Esau.

Finally, after twenty years, Jacob wanted to make peace with his brother, but he didn't know how Esau might react. Jacob gathered up his family to travel to where Esau lived. Jacob decided to offer Esau many presents and ask Esau to forgive him. When Esau heard Jacob was coming, he prepared for a battle. The night before reaching his brother, Jacob had a dream in which he wrestled with an angel, trying to figure out how to solve his problem with Esau.

The next day, Jacob's and Esau's soldiers approached each other, but they didn't fight. Esau ran to Jacob and hugged him. Then Jacob asked for forgiveness for what he had done years ago, and insisted that Esau accept the many presents Jacob had brought him. Esau accepted his apology and asked Jacob why he had decided to make peace after so many years. Jacob told Esau that while he was praying about what to do, he no longer saw Esau as an enemy, but saw "thy face, as though I had seen the face of God, and thou wast pleased with me" (Genesis 33:10).

Praying had helped Jacob see Esau not as an enemy, but in the way God would see him. At that moment, Jacob realized he and his brother could finally be at peace with each other.

Praying to see an enemy the way God sees them can make all the difference when we need to forgive or be forgiven by them.

Something to Think About
• Jacob wanted something so much he was willing to lie to his dad and cheat his brother in order to get it. It didn't work out too well for him. Have you ever wanted something that desperately?

"If a man say, I love God, and hateth his brother, he is a liar: for he that loveth not his brother whom he hath seen, how can he love God whom he hath not seen?"
(I John 4:20)

BIBLE MORALS FOR CHILDREN

"[The prodigal son would] have filled his belly with the husks
that the swine did eat: ...."
(Luke 15:16)

FORGIVENESS

THE PRODIGAL SON — YOU CAN GO HOME AGAIN

Luke: 15

Jesus told a parable, an earthly story with a heavenly message, of a man who had two sons. The older son was obedient, made good choices, and did everything he was supposed to do. The younger son didn't behave the same way. He didn't want to live a responsible life with his family anymore. He asked his dad to give him the inheritance he was promised to receive when he was older.

The younger son took the money, left home, spent the money on wasteful things, and soon had nothing left. Life was then extremely difficult for the young man. The only job he could get was feeding pigs on a farm. At times when he was starving, he thought about eating the pigs' food. One day, it occurred to him that even his dad's servants lived better than he did. He decided to return home, apologize to his dad, and ask if he could work as one of the servants. The young man began the journey back to his home. When he came near his house, his dad who was joyful to see him again, threw a party to celebrate his homecoming and let him work on their farm once again.

During the party, the older son returned to the house after another hard day working for the family. The older son got angry when he saw the party and how generously his dad was treating the brother who had done nothing but waste his money. The older son told his dad that he had always done what he was supposed to do, yet his dad had never thrown a party for him. Instead, the dad was throwing a party for the lazy, wasteful, and selfish younger brother!

The dad explained to his older son why he gave the party for the younger one. "Son, thou art ever with me, and all that I have is thine. It was meet that we should make merry, and be glad: for this thy brother was dead, and is alive again; and was lost, and is found" (Luke 15:31–32).

The dad told his older son there was no need to be angry because he would inherit everything someday. It was right to celebrate the younger son's homecoming because he was safe and had finally started living a responsible life.

No matter how wasteful, or *prodigal*, we are, and no matter how badly we mess up our own lives, God is *always* there to love and forgive us. He *always* offers us a chance to start over. It doesn't mean we have nothing to worry about or nothing to fix when we do wrong. It means that it's never too late to start doing the right thing with our lives.

Something to Think About
- What's the hardest thing you were ever asked to forgive? Did you?
- What's one of the biggest changes you've made or would like to make in your life?
- Have you ever been jealous of a brother or sister? How did you deal with it?

"And be ye kind one to another, tenderhearted, forgiving one another, even as God for Christ's sake hath forgiven you."
(Ephesians 4:32)

"And when they were come to the place, which is called Calvary, there they crucified him, ..."
(Luke 23:33)

FORGIVENESS

THE CRUCIFIXION: WHAT DID JESUS SAY?

Matthew: 18, Luke: 23

How many times should we forgive someone who continues to wrong us? Is there a point when it's okay to tell someone we won't ever forgive them? Are there people who do such terrible things that they don't deserve to be forgiven? Two examples of forgiveness from the life of Jesus Christ have been considered the way we should follow when deciding when, or if, to forgive someone.

Example #1: Forgiving Someone 490 Times!
Jesus was with his disciples one day when Peter asked him how many times a good person should forgive someone else. Peter guessed seven times. He thought this was a good number because Jewish law only required you to forgive someone three times. Jesus' answer surprised Peter. Jesus told him we should forgive someone 70 TIMES 7 or 490 times! Was Jesus saying we should count up to 490 and then stop forgiving the person on the 491st time they wronged us? Or, was he was saying we should forgive others without limit?

Example #2: The Crucifixion of Jesus
When Jesus was crucified on the cross, it was the most horrible, painful way to execute someone. But right in the middle of what seemed to be the end of Jesus' life, suffering unimaginable cruelty, Jesus was willing to forgive. He called out to God, and said something completely unexpected.

You might guess Jesus would have asked God to destroy the people who were wrongfully killing him, but he didn't. Instead, Jesus said, "Father, forgive them; for they know not what they do …" (Luke 23:34).

Any time we are wronged or treated terribly, we, like Jesus, can know that the people trying to harm us need to be forgiven. If they knew better, they would do better. We hurt ourselves when we refuse to forgive. God says wrongdoers will not go unpunished.

Something to Think About
• Jesus said we should forgive everything. Is there anything you wouldn't be willing to forgive?

BIBLE MORALS FOR CHILDREN

Yea, though I walk through the valley of the shadow of death, I will fear no evil: for thou art with me; ...."
(Psalms 23:4)

Chapter 6

OVERCOMING FEAR

TWO PSALMS (SONGS) TO MAKE YOU FEEL SAFE
Psalm 23, Psalm 91

No one wants to be afraid, but fear challenges people more than anything else. The Bible gives us many examples for how to overcome our fears.

The book of Psalms is the largest book in the Bible with 150 chapters! The word *psalm* means song, and about half of these songs are thought to have been written by King David. The psalms had a variety of purposes, including: singing God's praise, asking God to help communities that were suffering, and individuals asking God to help them personally. The psalms express confidence in God's ability and willingness to provide whatever help is necessary and whenever it is needed.

Psalm 23
The first verse of this chapter offers a wonderful explanation for why we never need be afraid, "The LORD is my shepherd; I shall not want" (Psalm 23:1). This psalm describes all mankind as sheep who are always provided for and protected by the greatest, most powerful *shepherd*, God. It tells us that when we come upon dangerous situations — even if we end up right in the middle of all our enemies — God never leaves us. "Yea, though I walk through the valley of the shadow of death, I will fear no evil: for thou art with me; ..." (Psalm 23:4). The psalm ends with confidence that we can count on God to keep us safe and meet all our needs, forever and wherever.

Psalm 91
This chapter is believed to have been written by Moses and has a different feeling than Psalm 23. It also talks about God's constant protection, but it goes into much more detail about what kinds of things God protects us from. These

things include: people trying to harm us, wild animals, sickness, and even fear of the dark. "For he shall give his angels charge over thee, to keep thee in all thy ways" (Psalms 91:11).

Psalm 91 emphasizes God's protection, resulting from loving and obeying God with all our hearts. The Psalm promises that if we stay close to God, he will cover us with his protecting love like a mother bird protects her babies. We can trust God to keep us and our homes completely safe.

FEAR'S ANTIDOTE

I John 4:18

In two words, *perfect love*, the Bible offers the guaranteed antidote to fear of all kinds. "There is no fear in love; but perfect love casteth out fear: ..." (I John 4:18).

An antidote is something that immediately takes away the power of anything harmful. The Bible's two words, *perfect love*, describe the kind of love God has for us. It's the love we're supposed to have for him and each other. When we are willing to forgive and love our enemies, we lose our fear of them. When we realize that God's love is all powerful, always present, and always providing everything we need, we stop fearing that *anything* could possibly harm us. We stop fearing we won't have enough friends or money. We stop worrying about our health or being harmed in accidents. We stop fearing we won't know what to say or do in a challenging situation. We have less and less fear of everything as we practice having more perfect love for God and each other.

Something to Think About
- Who's someone you feel safe with? What qualities do they have that make you feel safe?
- What's the most afraid you've ever been? How did you deal with it?

"I will say of the LORD, He is my refuge and my fortress: my God; in him will I trust."
(Psalms 91:2)

BIBLE MORALS FOR CHILDREN

"*[And Peter] walked on the water, to go to Jesus.*
(Matthew 14:29)

OVERCOMING FEAR

LOSING FEAR: WALKING ON WATER

Matthew: 14

One day, Jesus finished preaching to a large crowd. He told his disciples to start sailing their boat across the Sea of Galilee, and he'd join them later. After the disciples had sailed for a while, it became dark, and the sea became rough from strong winds.

The disciples looked out over the water and saw a human figure walking on the sea! They were terrified because they thought it was an evil spirit approaching their boat. But it was Jesus, and he called to his disciples telling them there was nothing to fear. Peter, one of Jesus' disciples, called out to Jesus: "Lord, if it be thou, bid me come unto thee on the water. And he said, Come. And when Peter was come down out of the ship, he walked on the water, to go to Jesus" (Matthew 14:28–29).

Jesus told Peter to walk out to him. Then Peter walked a few steps on the water, but when he looked at the wind and waves, he got scared and started to sink! Jesus reached out to give his hand to Peter and told him he should never have doubted him. Almost immediately, they were back in the boat with the other disciples. The sea calmed down, and even the wind stopped blowing.

What a story! We might never try to walk on water, but there will be many times in our lives when we want to accomplish something that seems scary or impossible. When Peter focused on being obedient, walking on the water to go to Jesus, he had no fear and no problems. It wasn't until he started thinking more about his own fear and limitations that Peter began to sink.

If we let ourselves focus more on our fears than on the good we're trying to accomplish, then we also start to *sink* or fall short of our goals. The Bible gives much proof that when we forget about our own fears and focus on trusting and obeying God, we can accomplish anything!

Something to Think About
- What's something you never thought you'd be able to do, but did? What made it possible?
- What's something you'd like to be able to do, but can't imagine how?

BIBLE MORALS FOR CHILDREN

"And the children of Israel went into the midst of the sea upon the dry ground: .... And the Egyptians pursued, and went in after them to the midst of the sea, even all Pharaoh's horses, his chariots, and his horsemen."
(Exodus 14:22–23)

Chapter 7

LOOKING FOR THE PROMISED LAND

PARTING OF THE RED SEA

Exodus: 14

The Hebrews had been slaves of Pharaoh and the Egyptians for hundreds of years. The Hebrews prayed for God's help, and Pharaoh decided to let the Hebrews go free. They quickly gathered their possessions and headed out into the desert before Pharaoh changed his mind. Moses led the thousands of Hebrews to the Promised Land across the desert.

God told Moses and the Hebrews to walk toward the Red Sea on their way to the Promised Land. As they approached the Red Sea, the Hebrews looked back in the direction from which they'd come and saw a huge dust cloud that terrified them! Pharaoh, once again, had changed his mind about letting the Hebrews go free, so he was chasing after them with thousands of soldiers and chariots.

Moses kept leading the Hebrews straight toward the Red Sea. To slow down the Egyptian army, God placed a pillar of clouds between the Hebrews and the soldiers during the day, and a pillar of fire during the night. The clouds and fire were so thick the soldiers were forced to slow down. This allowed the Hebrews to reach the shore of the Red Sea, but how would they get across the water?

The Hebrews cried out to Moses that they would all be killed because they were trapped between the Red Sea and the Egyptian soldiers! With total trust and faith in God, Moses gave the Hebrews hope: "Fear ye not, stand still, and see the salvation of the LORD, which he will shew to you to-day: for the Egyptians whom ye have seen to-day, ye shall see them again no more for ever" (Exodus 14:13).

That night, a strong wind blew on the Red Sea and pushed the water apart, so the Hebrews were able to walk across the bottom of the sea. When the Egyptians finally saw through the pillars of fire and clouds, they could see the Hebrews escaping. The Egyptians drove their chariots straight into the dry sea to catch the Hebrews. Part way across, God caused the Egyptians to have problems with their chariots' wheels, and they were slowed down in chasing the Hebrews. By the time all of the Egyptians were in the dry sea bed making the crossing, the last of the Hebrews were reaching dry land on the other side of the sea. God told Moses to wave his hand over the waters. When he did, the sea closed back and all of the Egyptian soldiers drowned. The Hebrews escaped Pharaoh's army and continued their 40-year journey to the Promised Land.

How did the Hand of God part the Red Sea? Could it have been an extremely low tide that had returned rapidly? Was the Red Sea a nearby and much shallower body of water called the Reed Sea? Or did this miraculous event happen exactly as the Bible describes? We'll never know for sure. Regardless of the exact details about the Hebrews' escape from the Egyptians, the real message and usefulness of this Bible story remain. When we control our fear and maintain our faith that all things are possible with God, we can trust him to protect us. He will always direct us to safety, no matter how challenging our problems seem to be or how long the journey.

Something to Think About
- If someone suggests a new way of doing something, are you usually willing to try it, or do you insist on doing things your way?

"Ah Lord GOD! behold, thou hast made the heaven and the earth by thy great power and stretched out arm, and there is nothing too hard for thee:"
(Jeremiah 32:17)

BIBLE MORALS FOR CHILDREN

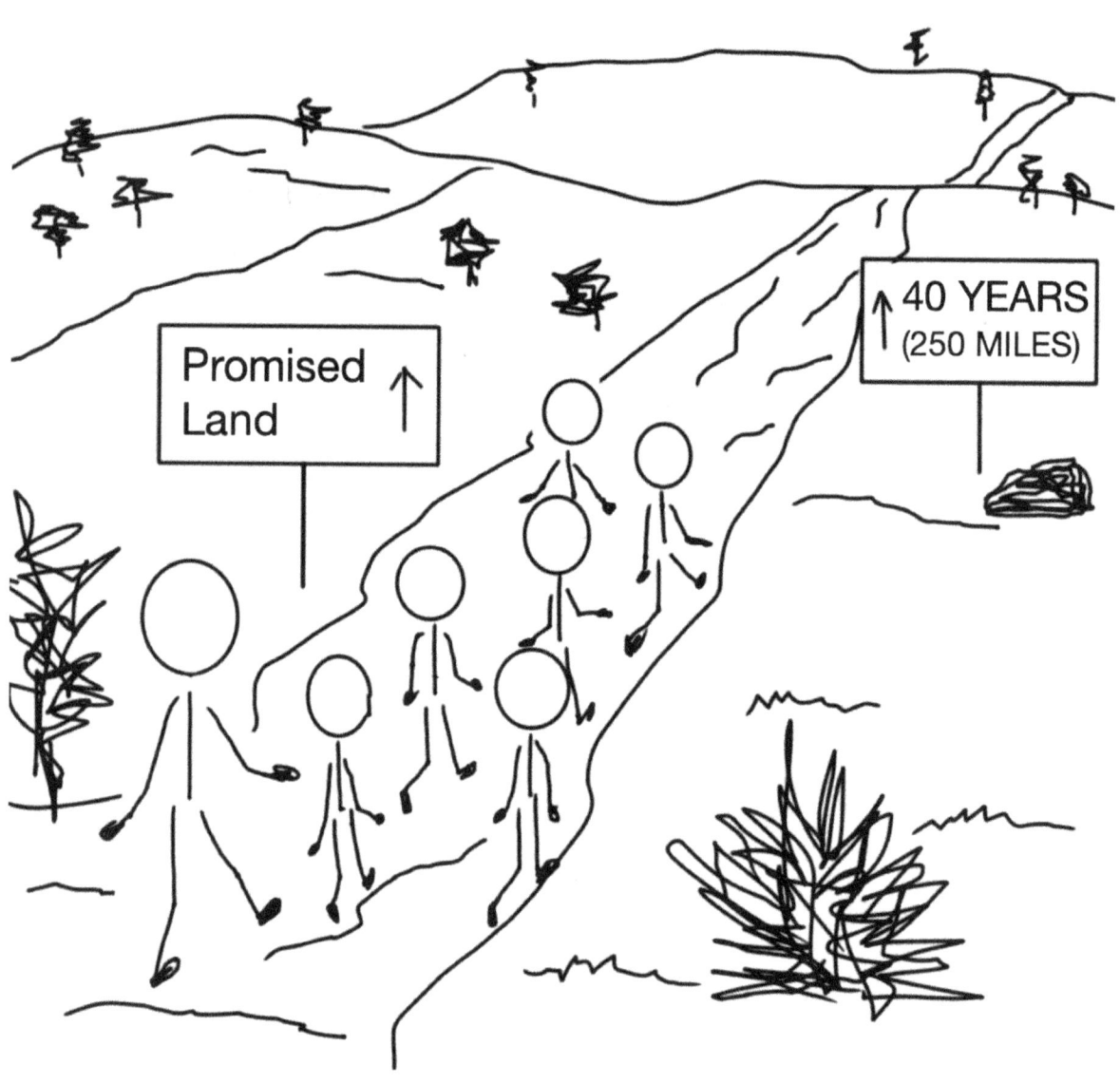

"And the LORD'S anger was kindled against Israel, and he made them wander in the wilderness forty years, ..."
(Numbers 32:13)

LOOKING FOR THE PROMISED LAND

40 YEARS TO WALK 250 MILES

Nehemiah 9, Exodus 9, 10, 13, 16,17

God had always told the Hebrews there was a Promised Land waiting for them across the desert. Serving as slaves to the Egyptians for hundreds of years, the Hebrews finally couldn't take it any longer. They prayed to God to rescue them from the Egyptians, so they could walk across the desert to the Promised Land.

Moses, a Hebrew leader, went to Pharaoh, the Egyptian leader, and told him, "Let my people go, ..." (Exodus 5:1). He wanted Pharaoh to free the Hebrews from the Egyptians who held them as slaves. Pharaoh agreed several times to let them go free, but then changed his mind and went back on his word. Every time Pharaoh broke his promise to give the Hebrews their freedom, God sent a different plague on the Egyptians, including hordes of flies and locusts, frogs, boils all over their bodies, and turning their drinking water to blood.

Pharaoh begged Moses for each plague to stop. Pharaoh said he would allow the Hebrews leave Egypt, but every time, he would break his word. Finally, the worst plague was sent to the Egyptians. Their firstborn sons all died overnight. This horror finally convinced Pharaoh to let the Hebrews leave Egypt to search for the Promised Land. "[Pharaoh] called for Moses and Aaron by night, and said, Rise up, and get you forth from among my people, both ye and the children of Israel; and go, serve the LORD, ..." (Exodus 12:31).

Thousands of the freed Hebrews, led by Moses, began their journey across the desert, a distance of about 250 miles. The trip should have taken less than three weeks, but it ended up taking forty *years* because God kept punishing the Hebrews for disobeying him and losing their faith. Numerous problems happened along the way. The biggest problem was how to provide food and water for the thousands of Hebrews walking across the desert.

When food began to run out, the Hebrews began to rebel against their leader, Moses. God told Moses that he would provide breakfast and dinner every day for all the Hebrews, and he *did*, for forty years! Every morning, there was a thin layer of edible material on the ground that the Hebrews called *manna*, or bread from heaven. Every night, enough quail dropped into their camp to feed everyone. God wanted to make sure the Hebrews were acknowledging him and not themselves as the source of this food, so he told them to collect only enough food each morning and evening to feed themselves for that day. When some of the Hebrews became afraid that there wouldn't be enough food, they tried to collect extra to save, but it rotted.

Then, there was the worry about having enough water. On one occasion, God told Moses to get the needed water out of a rock in the desert. Moses struck the rock and enough water poured out of it to meet all of the Hebrews' needs.

Last, but not least, the Hebrews took only the clothes they were wearing when they left Egypt. The Bible says that 40 years later, the clothes themselves were not even worn out! Each step of the way for those 40 years, the Hebrews were led safely through the wilderness to the Promised Land. God's message to them never changed: trust him, obey his Word, and all their needs would be met. Over three thousand years later, as we try to find our way through our *own* wilderness experiences, God still sends us the same message.

Something to Think About
- When a group activity doesn't go the way you planned, do you stick with the goal and support the group, or do you tend to blame others and give up?
- What's the longest you've worked toward achieving a goal?

"Have not I commanded thee? Be strong and of a good courage; be not afraid, neither be thou dismayed: for the LORD thy God is with thee whithersoever thou goest."
(Joshua 1:9)

BIBLE MORALS FOR CHILDREN

"Jonah was in the belly of the fish three days and three nights."
(Jonah 1:17)

Chapter 8

BE GOOD AND OBEY GOD ... OR ELSE!

Jesus's said, "Ye shall know the truth, and truth shall make you free" (John 8:32). It is one of the Bible's most well-known statements, but what happens when we don't tell the truth? What happens when we lie or knowingly disobey God's Word? The Bible says nothing good comes from choosing to do either of those things. Sometimes, it means losing our freedom. Sometimes, being untruthful makes us lose much more.

JONAH SWALLOWED BY A HUGE FISH

Jonah: 1–3

One day, a Hebrew named Jonah heard God telling him to go to a town called Nineveh to tell the people to stop acting so wickedly, or God would destroy their city. Jonah didn't want to go to Nineveh because their people were enemies of the Hebrews. Instead, Jonah got on a ship traveling to a different city called Tarshish to hide from God. While the boat was at sea, a great storm came up that threatened to destroy the ship. The sailors believed God was causing the storm because he was angry with someone on the ship, but they didn't know who it was. Jonah admitted that he was the one who had disobeyed God. He told the sailors that the way to save themselves was to throw him overboard. They did!

The sea immediately calmed down, and the Bible says God sent a huge fish to swallow Jonah. During the three days Jonah was in the fish's belly, he asked God to forgive him and promised he would do better if God gave him another chance. God did. He made the fish swim to shore where it spit Jonah out onto the beach. Then, for the second time, God told Jonah to travel to Nineveh to tell the people to stop living so wickedly. This time, Jonah obeyed. "So Jonah arose, and went unto Nineveh, according to the word of the LORD" (Jonah 3:3).

He told the people of Nineveh they'd be destroyed in forty days if they didn't change their wicked ways. They believed him and changed their behavior, so God saved Nineveh as he promised!

Many stories in the Bible emphasize the idea of God giving us second chances. In Jonah's situation, he was given the second opportunity he had begged God to give him. When Jonah finally delivered God's message to the people of Nineveh, they, too, took advantage of the second chance God had given them and were saved.

Something to Think About
• When you've done something wrong, do you always take responsibility for what you've done, or do you avoid taking responsibility?
• Sometimes when we pray to God for an answer to a problem, he doesn't give us the answer we wanted. Has this happened to you?

"Whither shall I go from thy spirit? or whither shall I flee from thy presence? If I ascend up into heaven, thou art there: if I make my bed in hell, behold, thou art there. If I take the wings of the morning, and dwell in the uttermost parts of the sea; Even there shall thy hand lead me, and thy right hand shall hold me."
(Psalms 139:7–10)

BIBLE MORALS FOR CHILDREN

"Then the LORD rained upon Sodom and upon Gomorrah brimstone and fire from the LORD out of heaven;"
(Genesis 19:24)

BE GOOD AND OBEY GOD … OR ELSE!

THE DESTRUCTION OF SODOM AND GOMORRAH

Genesis: 18, 19

Sodom and Gomorrah were considered two of the most wicked cities on earth because the people living there had no respect for sexual morality. God saw that the cities were very sinful, so he decided to destroy them. The Hebrew leader, Abraham, asked God to spare the cities. Abraham thought that there were at least *some* righteous people living there, including his nephew, Lot, and his family.

Abraham offered God a deal. Would God spare Sodom and Gomorrah if Abraham could find 50 righteous men in those cities? God accepted the offer. "And the LORD said, If I find in Sodom fifty righteous within the city, then I will spare all the place for their sakes" (Genesis 18: 26).

But Lot couldn't find 50 righteous men. Abraham then asked God if he would save the cities if he could find 45 righteous men. God agreed, but again, Lot could not find 45 righteous men. Abraham's conversation with God continued in this way until God's final offer was that he would save Sodom and Gomorrah if Lot could find just ten righteous men. Unfortunately, the cities were too wicked, and Lot could not find even ten good men.

God then sent two angels to Sodom and Gomorrah to tell Lot to leave town with his family because God was going to destroy both cities. Lot had the angels spend that night at his house, but Sodom and Gomorrah's residents were evil. They tried to break into Lot's home to harm the two angels. That was enough for the angels! To keep this violent mob from breaking into Lot's home that night and assaulting them, the angels made many of the violent mob blind.

The next morning, the angels told Lot and his family to leave town immediately. They gave Lot a serious warning. They told him to not look back at Sodom and Gomorrah at all, but to keep looking straight ahead in the direction of the town where they were going. As Lot and his family were leaving town, God started sending a fire storm down upon the two cities until they completely burned down. As Lot and his family were leaving, his wife's curiosity became too great, and she disobeyed the angels' command. She turned around to look back at the two cities being destroyed, and the Bible says she was immediately turned into a pillar of salt.

There are several theories why Lot's wife was punished. Did she turn around because she didn't want to leave the wicked city? Did she think she didn't have to obey God's Word?

When we find ourselves in an environment with people who are doing wrong things, we can stay safe by removing ourselves from those situations as quickly as possible, and not letting ourselves be tempted to return to them.

Something to Think About
• When your friends are doing wrong things, do you go along with them because they're your friends? Do you remove yourself from the situation? Or, do you try to change their minds about what they are doing?

"Be not deceived; God is not mocked: for whatsoever a man soweth, that shall he also reap."
(Galatians 6:7)

"[David] saw a woman washing herself; and the woman was very beautiful to look upon."
(II Samuel 11:2)

BE GOOD AND OBEY GOD ... OR ELSE!

DAVID AND BATHSHEBA — EVERYTHING WASN'T ENOUGH

II Samuel 11, 12

King David was considered the greatest of all the kings of Israel. Handsome, an excellent musician, a brave warrior, and a skilled military leader, David went through many challenges and overcame them all. He was blessed by God with all the power, fame, and money anyone could desire, and David repeatedly proclaimed his loyalty to and love for God.

But David wanted more. At the peak of his power, he made a mistake that cost him much. While relaxing one night on the roof of his palace in Jerusalem, he looked out over the city and saw a beautiful woman named Bathsheba bathing on her rooftop. David sent a messenger to bring her to his palace even though he had seven other wives. He also knew that the woman was married to one of his army officers. David committed adultery with Bathsheba, and she became pregnant.

David wanted to marry Bathsheba, so he arranged for her husband, one of his own army officers, to be killed in battle. Afterwards, a prophet named Nathan went to see David to tell him that God was angry with him for what he had done. David knew he had done something terribly wrong, "And David said unto Nathan, I have sinned against the LORD" (II Samuel 12:13).

The rest of David's life had much pain and sorrow. His baby son from Bathsheba died. His kingdom had a civil war, and one of his sons fought against him. Finally, a terrible disease killed thousands of his fellow Hebrews. David had little peace or joy for the rest of his life because he had disobeyed God. Gratitude, obedience to God, and humility would have protected David. These qualities still protect us today.

Something to Think About
- Have you ever stolen anything? How did it make you feel? Did you go back and admit what you had done, or did you do nothing?
- In God's Ten Commandments, why do you think stealing is considered just as serious as killing someone or not believing in God?

BIBLE MORALS FOR CHILDREN

*"But thou, when you prayest, enter into thy closet,
and when thou hast shut thy door,
pray to thy Father which is in secret; ...."
(Matthew 6:6)*

Chapter 9

HOW DO YOU PRAY?

THE LORD'S PRAYER

Matthew 6

What does it mean when we say we are going to *pray*? It means we want to communicate with God, but there are many different ideas about how a person can pray.

Some people believe that praying is talking out loud to God or thinking silently about him. Others believe that praying is mainly about asking God for things like money, protection, health, or a job. Thanking God for what he has already provided is another way people pray.

Jesus' disciples asked him to teach them how to pray. He taught them both *what* to pray and *how* to do it. He kept it simple. Jesus said *not* to make a public spectacle out of prayer. Jesus taught that praying is communication between God and you. He said to find a private place, away from everyone else, and then you're ready to pray.

The prayer Jesus taught his disciples has come to be known as The LORD'S *Prayer*, and is found in the Bible's 6th chapter of Matthew, verses 9–13:

"Our Father which are in heaven, Hallowed be thy name."
The Lord's prayer starts by honoring God's name and referring to him as everyone's father which reminds us that we are all brothers and sisters.

"Thy kingdom come. Thy will be done in earth, as it is in heaven."
It continues by saying that God is the God of earth, as much as heaven, and needs to be obeyed right here and now.

"Give us this day our daily bread."
Next, the Lord's Prayer trusts God to care for us forever, but it asks him to supply our needs just one day at a time.

"And forgive us our debts, as we forgive our debtors."
The prayer follows by saying that if *we* want to be forgiven for wrong things we do to others, then we must forgive *others* when they wrong us.

"And lead us not into temptation, but deliver us from evil: For thine is the kingdom, and the power, and the glory, for ever. Amen."
The Lord's Prayer finishes by asking God to not let us be tempted to do wrong things, and acknowledges him as infinite, limitless, and everywhere. It establishes God as All-Powerful, as the One who should receive *all* credit for everything in his wonderful creation.

People often say *amen* at the end of The Lord's Prayer or other prayers. The word *amen* means *truth* or *certainty*. When a person says amen at the end of a prayer, they are reminding themselves that everything they have been saying or knowing about God is true and can be trusted forever.

Sometimes when we pray, we might have doubts. Is God even listening to us? How quickly will he respond to our prayers? God gives us a reassuring promise that he hears us, and loves us, and cares for us more than we could ever imagine. And God said, "And it shall come to pass, that before they call, I will answer; and while they are yet speaking, I will hear" (Isaiah 65:24).

Something to Think About
- When you pray to God, do you think it's better to tell him what you want, or is it better to listen to what he tells you?
- Why would someone say "thank you" at the *beginning* of their prayer?

"After this manner therefore pray ye:
Our Father which art in heaven,
Hallowed be thy name.
Thy kingdom come,
Thy will be done in earth, as it is in heaven.
Give us this day our daily bread.
And forgive us our debts, as we forgive our debtors.
And lead us not into temptation, but deliver us from evil:
For thine is the kingdom, and the power,
and the glory, for ever. Amen."
(Matthew 6:9–13)

BIBLE MORALS FOR CHILDREN

*And the devil said to Jesus, "All these things will I give thee,
if thou wilt fall down and worship me."
(Matthew 4:9)*

Chapter 10

JESUS

OVERCOMING THE BIGGEST TEMPTATIONS

Matthew: 4

After Jesus had been baptized, he was ready to start healing people and preaching God's Word. To prepare even more, he went out into the wilderness and fasted for forty days. Can you imagine not eating for forty days? What a way to test himself to see if he was spiritually and physically strong enough to stand up to all the temptations and challenges he was going to face in the next few years! At the end of the forty days, the devil showed up and tempted Jesus in three areas, the same three areas we all face in our own lives.

The first temptation is loving ourselves and material things more than God. Knowing Jesus was hungry after having no food for almost six weeks, the devil told Jesus he should turn desert rocks into bread, so Jesus could eat. Jesus refused the devil's offer because eating would have broken his fast. Jesus refused to believe that the solution to our problems is more food, money, or any material thing. He told the devil that the way to overcome these temptations is to lean completely on God: "It is written, Man shall not live by bread alone, but by every word that proceedeth out of the mouth of God" (Matthew 4:4).

The second temptation is pride. The devil took Jesus to the top of a tall temple and dared him to jump off. If Jesus was truly the Son of God, the devil told him, then angels would save him, and he'd wouldn't be hurt. The devil appealed to Jesus' pride, trying to make Jesus show off. Jesus refused and said that God always protects us, but we shouldn't go out of our way to do something dangerous to impress others.

The third temptation is human power. The devil took Jesus to the top of a tall mountain where he could see all of the towns and people below him. The devil said that if Jesus would worship him, then everything Jesus could see from the mountaintop would be his. Think of how much power and wealth that would have been! Jesus refused to worship the devil and told him that God is the only one we are to worship.

What happened with the devil after Jesus refused to give in to temptation? He disappeared! Jesus went on to live a life that changed the world. In our lives, when we stand *with* God and *against* temptations of materiality, pride, and personal power, we can expect the same results Jesus experienced. We can prove our total dominion over evil and our God-given ability to do good things with our lives.

When we read this story in the Bible, we see that when Jesus refused the temptations, he answered the devil every time with a quote from the Bible stating, "It is written ..." (Matthew 4). In the toughest situations, Jesus himself found the immediate strength and support he needed from God's Word. We can, too!

Something to Think About
- Which of Jesus' three temptations have you had to deal with the most?
- Have you overcome temptations, or have they overcome you?

"God is faithful, who will not suffer you to be tempted above that ye are able; but will with the temptation also make a way to escape, that ye may be able to bear it."
(I Corinthians 10:13)

WANT TO BE HAPPY?

"For whosoever will save his life shall lose it: and whosoever will lose his life for my sake shall find it."
(Matthew 16:25)

Chapter 11

WANT TO BE HAPPY AND HAVE EVERYTHING?

We all want to be happy. We often look for happiness by trying to please ourselves. Most people have discovered that the more time they spend on themselves and the less time they spend helping others, the less happy they become. What advice does the Bible offer about finding happiness?

FORGET YOURSELF

Matthew: 10

"He that findeth his life shall lose it: and he that loseth his life for my sake shall find it" (Matthew 10:39). Jesus taught that if our main focus is on making our own lives happy with the things we do and buy, we will never find true happiness. He said the way to find happiness in our own lives is to forget about ourselves. Instead, we need to focus on doing what the Bible teaches, and that's helping other people find happiness and purpose in *their* lives.

Something to Think About
Put this Bible promise to the test! The next time you're feeling unhappy or dissatisfied, try forgetting your own problems, and go do something kind for someone else. Jesus said it would make *us* feel better. Try it and see!

BIBLE MORALS FOR CHILDREN

*"But seek ye first the kingdom of God, and his righteousness;
and all these things shall be added unto you."*
(Matthew 6:33)

WANT TO BE HAPPY AND HAVE EVERYTHING?
PUT GOD FIRST!

Matthew: 6

The Bible teaches that if we *first* look for our own happiness, and then *second*, worry about the things God tells us to do, we will *not* find happiness.

Jesus said we must reverse that order if we want to find lasting happiness. He said the first thing we should do is to pursue all the qualities God wants us to express in our lives: unselfishness, purity, forgiveness, kindness, moral courage, and love for others. If we make God's commands our first priority, Jesus promised that everything we need will come into our lives. If we try to do it the other way around, our own needs won't be filled. First things first!

Something to Think About
- One way to start your day is to get up in the morning, start doing all the things *you* want to do, and then ask God for help when you run into problems. The other way to start each day is to sit down, quietly pray, read the Bible for a few minutes, and listen to what God wants you to do. Compare which one gives you better results in your day.

BIBLE MORALS FOR CHILDREN

*"Thou wilt keep him in perfect peace,
whose mind is stayed on thee: ...."*
(Isaiah 26:3)

WANT TO BE HAPPY AND HAVE EVERYTHING?

THINK ON THESE THINGS!

Philippians: 4

Our lives are shaped by what we think. If we want happy lives, the Bible teaches that we must consistently focus our thinking on the right things. The Bible helps us by listing what some of those *right things* are. "Finally, brethren, whatsoever things are true, whatsoever things are honest, whatsoever things are just, whatsoever things are pure, whatsoever things are lovely, whatsoever things are of good report; if there be any virtue, and if there be any praise, think on these things" (Philippians 4:8).

Practice makes perfect. Keeping our focus on the qualities listed in Philippians 4:8 is what brings true happiness.

Something to Think About
Default thoughts are the things we think about over and over when we're not concentrating.

- What are your default thoughts?
- Are your present thoughts bringing you happiness?
- Would changing your thoughts improve your life?

BIBLE MORALS FOR CHILDREN

*"Moreover if thy brother shall trespass against thee,
go and tell him his fault between thee and him alone:
if he shall hear thee, thou has gained thy brother."*
(Matthew 18:15)

Chapter 12

THE MATTHEW PRINCIPLE

SOLVING PROBLEMS WITH OTHERS

Matthew: 18

"Moreover if thy brother shall trespass against thee, go and tell him his fault between thee and him alone: if he shall hear thee, thou has gained thy brother" (Matthew 18:15).

We have all experienced angry or hurt feelings that won't go away when we believe someone has harmed us. If we don't solve problems like these, then unhappy feelings build up inside us, or we explode in anger. Neither of these choices are good because they usually make things worse. The Bible includes a three-step method for solving problems with others. This method, taught by Jesus, is found in the book of Matthew and is often called *The Matthew Principle*.

Step 1: Go directly to the person you have a disagreement with and talk it over without anyone else.
This is something many of us never do. It's more tempting and much easier to go to a third party and complain to them, but there is a problem with that plan. It doesn't work. Going directly to the person you're upset with is the best way to quickly resolve a problem because it prevents the disagreement from getting more serious. It also enables you to maintain a peaceful future relationship with the person involved. If Step 1 doesn't work, go to Step 2.

Step 2: Take one or two other people with you to talk to the person with whom you have a disagreement.
People who are not directly involved in a disagreement can often share some thoughts that can lead you to a solution. If Step 2 doesn't work, go to Step 3.

Step 3: Pursue a more public solution.
The Matthew Principle finally says that if the first two attempts to privately

solve the problem haven't worked, you have every right to pursue a more public solution. Depending on your situation, this third step can be useful, but not when it's your first step.

Here's why a one-on-one conversation should be your *first* step, and talking publicly about the problem your *last* step. It gives both people a chance to apologize for what they said or did that was wrong or hurtful. It gives both parties the opportunity to avoid public humiliation or embarrassment. Best of all, it leaves both people in a better position to resolve future disagreements if they occur.

Something to Think About
• If you made a list of all the people you don't like or who make you angry, how long would the list be? You have everything to gain and nothing to lose by choosing one of those people on your list, applying the Matthew Principle, and seeing if it solves the problem. If it does, you might try it on all of the people on your list.

"Speak ye every man the truth to his neighbour;"
(Zechariah 8:16)

BIBLE MORALS FOR CHILDREN

"And when he was come out of the ship, immediately there met him out of the tombs a man with an unclean spirit, Who had his dwelling among the tombs; and no man could bind him, no, not with chains:"
(Mark 5:2–3)

Chapter 13

CAN GOD HEAL EVERYTHING?

One of the things about the Bible that interests many people is its amazing examples of healing, over 70 in total. The Bible describes complete and usually immediate healings of mental and physical problems that were thought to be hopeless. The most significant part of the healings is that they were accomplished by prayer alone. The following are three examples found in the Bible.

HEALING MENTAL ILLNESS — A MAN AND A HERD OF PIGS

Mark: 5

Jesus and his disciples landed their boat in a city called Gadara. They were near a cemetery when a violently insane man who lived in the cemetery suddenly confronted Jesus. The man was well known for his dangerous and scary behavior. He would run around naked, crying and cutting himself with rocks. He was so violent and crazy he broke the chains that the local residents used to try to control him.

When the insane man saw Jesus, he ran up to him and told Jesus he knew who he was. The insane man said he didn't want to be tormented. He wanted to be left alone, but Jesus wasn't going to let the man continue to live in such a horrible situation. The Bible says Jesus didn't speak directly to the man but instead spoke to the mental illness that was controlling him. Jesus called the mental illness a *devil*.

Jesus asked the devil to tell him his name, or identify the mental illness's name. The devil said it wasn't just one mental illness, but many! Jesus knew the man had a God-given right to be healed, so he commanded all of the devils to leave the man and enter into a herd of pigs.

The man's crazy behavior stopped immediately, but then the herd of pigs began acting as if the devils had entered them! "And the unclean spirits went out, and entered into the swine: and the herd ran violently down a steep place into the sea, (they were about two thousand;) and were choked in the sea" (Mark 5:13).

That was the end of the man's mental illness and crazy behavior and also the end of those pigs. After his time with Jesus, the man was able to be calm and normal. He put on clothes, sat and talked with Jesus, and decided to spend his life telling others about God's incredible power to heal anything.

Something to Think About
When people encounter homeless individuals talking wildly or begging, they usually ignore them or give them money. Neither approach helps the person in need.

- Have you ever tried asking a homeless person if they'd like you to pray for them, or talked to them about how much God loves them?
- If you were homeless, how would you want someone to interact with you?

"For God hath not given us the spirit of fear; but of power, and of love, and of a sound mind."
(II Timothy 1:7)

BIBLE MORALS FOR CHILDREN

"And he [Jesus] took the blind man by the hand, ...
spit on his eyes, and put his hands upon him, ..."
(Mark 8:23)
"and he was restored ...."
(Mark 8:25)

CAN GOD HEAL EVERYTHING?

HEALING BLINDNESS — WHAT DID SPIT HAVE TO DO WITH IT?

Mark: 8

Jesus had just arrived with his disciples in a town called Bethsaida when some local people took a blind man to Jesus. The blind man wanted to see.

Jesus agreed to heal him and walked away from the crowd with the man. Jesus then faced the man and spit on his eyes! Asking the blind man if he could see, the man told Jesus he could see a little bit, but not well. Then Jesus, "put his hands again upon his eyes [the man's] and made him look up: and he was restored, and saw every man clearly" (Mark 8:25). To reach a full understanding of this healing requires some serious thinking!

Why did Jesus spit on the man's eyes? Was there something special about Jesus' saliva? Here's another possibility.

In those days, if a Jew, as Jesus was, strongly disagreed with something that was being talked about, they might spit on the ground.

Jesus knew the Bible taught that everything God made was good. Blindness certainly wouldn't be considered good in any way. Was spitting on and touching the man's eyes Jesus' way of telling the man that God could not have caused it, and Jesus wouldn't allow himself or the blind man to believe that anymore? Did the man need to instead believe he could be healed because blindness couldn't possibly be any part of God's wonderful and good creation? We don't know for sure. What we do know is that when the man came to Jesus, he was blind. When he left Jesus, the blind man could see.

Something to Think About
- Have you ever prayed for God to heal you or someone else? What happened?

BIBLE MORALS FOR CHILDREN

"Then went he [Naaman] down, and dipped himself seven times in Jordan, according to the saying of the man of God: and his flesh came again like unto the flesh of a little child, and he was clean."
(II Kings 5:14)

CAN GOD HEAL EVERYTHING?

HEALING NAAMAN'S LEPROSY AND PRIDE

II Kings: 5

Naaman was head of the entire Syrian army and a national hero. Unfortunately, he had leprosy, a terrible and incurable disease of that time.

One day, one of the servant girls of Naaman's wife told her Naaman could be healed if he went to see Elisha, God's prophet in Israel. Naaman probably had to think carefully about that possibility. Naaman's country had conquered Israel, and he didn't believe in the One God that Israel's people worshipped. On the other hand, Naaman wanted to be healed. He probably decided he had nothing to lose by giving Elisha the opportunity to heal him.

Naaman and a group of his soldiers traveled to Elisha's house. Because he was an important man, Naaman thought Elisha would come outside of his house to greet him, conduct a great ceremony, and ask God to heal him. But that's not how it happened.

Elisha never even went outside to meet Naaman. Instead, Elisha sent his servant to tell Naaman what he must do if he wanted to be healed. "Go and wash in Jordan seven times, and thy flesh shall come again to thee, and thou shalt be clean" (II Kings 5:10). Dip himself in the Jordan River? Hearing the prophet's simple directions, Naaman was enraged!

Naaman said he would never wash himself in the Jordan River. It was a place where ordinary Hebrews took baths and washed their clothes. Naaman angrily left Elisha's house and headed back to Syria.

Naaman's servants begged him to follow Elisha's directions. They told him that if Elisha had asked him to do something difficult, he would have done it. Why would he not be willing to do something easy? The servants' reasoning changed Naaman's mind. He went to the Jordan River, dipped himself in it seven times, and was completely healed!

Was it the special healing powers of the water that healed Naaman, or was it his willingness to humbly listen to the Word of God, spoken by the prophet Elisha?

In the thousands of years since Naaman, countless people have continued to find healing in their own lives by humbling themselves before God.

BIBLE MORALS FOR CHILDREN

Something to Think About

When people are praised for doing something well, some of them take personal credit for it, while others are humble and say it is a blessing from God.

- How do you respond when people praise you?

"Humble yourselves therefore under the mighty hand of God, that he may exalt you in due time: Casting all your care upon him; for he careth for you."
(I Peter 5:6–7)

BIBLE MORALS FOR CHILDREN

*"Put on the whole armour of God, that ye may be able
to stand against the wiles of the devil."*
(Ephesians 6:11)

Chapter 14

YOU'RE SAFE ... IF YOU DON'T RUN AWAY

PUT ON THE WHOLE ARMOR OF GOD

Ephesians 6

If you want to live a good life, you must be willing to fight for it! Every day you try to be unselfish, honest, or fearless, you'll be attacked by the temptations to be selfish, dishonest, and afraid.

Fortunately, the Bible tells about *spiritual* armor that will protect us and is always available any time and place, but there's a catch. To be completely safe and protected in our daily fighting, we must put on the *whole* set of armor.

Before you read any farther, get a piece of paper and a pen.

Draw a large stick figure of a person who represents you as a spiritual warrior. As you read through the Bible descriptions of each piece of spiritual armor we must constantly wear, draw it on your stick warrior. Make sure you don't miss any pieces because this will be important at the end.

First, the Bible says to put on a wide belt representing truth. Always telling the truth holds everything together in our lives.

The second piece of spiritual armor is the breastplate representing righteousness. A breastplate covers the front chest area. A person who is *righteous* always tries to do the right thing.

Next, the Bible says to put on tall boots that represent peace. Anywhere we walk, we should have the goal of bringing peace.

A shield that represents faith is the next armor piece. A large shield can cover and protect most of the body in a battle. A strong faith can protect a person from many problems in their life.

The Bible calls the next-to-last piece of spiritual armor the *helmet of salvation*. Salvation means to save something. Maintaining pure, spiritual thoughts saves us from allowing negative, wrong, or fearful ideas from entering our thought and lives.

Our final protective piece of spiritual armor is the *sword of the Spirit* which represents the Word of God. The powerful teachings of the Bible — held in our hearts when trouble happens — give us the courage and ability to meet any challenge.

Now look at your stick-warrior drawing. See if you are *completely* protected and safe in your spiritual armor.

- Your helmet covers your head and neck.
- Your breastplate covers the whole front of your chest.
- Your wide belt of truth covers your middle area.
- Your tall boots cover your lower legs and feet, and your shield gives extra protection to the entire front of your body.
- Finally, your sword adds protection to any area in the front of your body.

Looking at your stick-warrior drawing, you might think you're completely protected by your armor, *but you're not!* The Bible doesn't describe any spiritual armor for your back!

The breastplate covers the front of your chest. How do we protect your back?

There's only one way: by always running *at* your problems, and never turning around and running *from* them! Now you're ready to protect yourself and defeat any problem that comes your way!

Something to Think About
- Think of a time when you avoided confronting a situation. If you had it to do over, would you do it differently?

"Fear ye not, stand still, and see the salvation of the LORD, which he will shew to you to-day: ...."
(Exodus 14:13)

"And the best of the three is love."
(The Message (MSG), I Corinthians 13:13)

Chapter 15

IS IT LOVE? TAKE THE TEST

WHAT DOES REAL LOVE LOOK LIKE? THE LOVE CHAPTER

I Corinthians: 13

Love is the one thing everyone wants most in their lives, yet it can be a confusing term. We often use the word *love* to express how much we like something. Pizza, swimming, a great song, a sunset, or a movie are examples of things we might *love*. We also say we love someone who is a great friend. Our deepest sense of love is usually toward our parents or someone we'd want to marry.

The thirteenth chapter of First Corinthians is known as the *Love Chapter* and is often read at wedding ceremonies. This chapter is famous because it goes into great detail describing what true love *is* — and what it isn't. Read this list to see how well you practice real love.

Love is more important than being extremely smart.

Love is more important than giving things to others and more important than having a lot of faith.

Love is patient, kind, and unselfish.

Love does NOT get angry at other people, and always thinks good things about them.

Love always hopes for and expects good things to happen. Love never gets upset when things it wants don't happen right away.

The Love Chapter ends by reminding us that many material things in life can be good and fun, but if they're not connected with real love, they don't last. Real love endures because it is not just *from* God, the Bible says Love *is* God. Love never fails, and it lasts forever!

How many of the true love qualities do you practice? Most people find that the more love qualities they practice, the happier their lives are.

Something to Think About

• Jesus said, "Greater love hath no man than this, that a man lay down his life for his friends" (King James Version, John 15:13). Jesus was saying that the greatest love we can have for someone is the willingness to sacrifice our life for theirs. Using his definition, how many people do you love?

"Greater love hath no man than this, that a man lay down his life for his friends."
(John 15:13)

BIBLE MORALS FOR CHILDREN

"Entreat me not to leave thee, or to return from following after thee: for whither thou goest, I will go; and where thou lodgest, I will lodge: thy people shall be my people, and thy God my God:"
(Ruth 1:16)

IS IT LOVE? TAKE THE TEST

AN EXAMPLE OF TRUE LOVE — THE STORY OF RUTH

Ruth: 1–4

If you like stories about pure, true love, the story of Ruth is for you.

Naomi, a woman from the city of Judea, had two sons. One son married Ruth, and the other son married Ruth's friend. They were all happy for about ten years until Naomi's husband, the sons' father, died. Naomi became a widow.

Shortly afterwards, Naomi's two sons also died. Now, Ruth, her friend, and Naomi were all widows without any way to support themselves! Naomi insisted that both of her daughters-in-law leave her and go back to where they originally lived in Moab, so they could find new husbands. Ruth's friend left right away, but Ruth refused to leave Naomi living by herself. She said the following words to Ruth. They are well-known and often read at weddings because they are such a pure example of true love.

"Entreat me not to leave thee, or to return from following after thee: for whither thou goest, I will go; and where thou lodgest, I will lodge: thy people shall be my people, and thy God my God:" (Ruth 1:16).

After a while, Naomi agreed to travel with Ruth to live in Naomi's hometown of Bethlehem. Ruth supported Naomi and herself by gleaning, cleaning up the leftovers after the grain fields were harvested. Ruth learned that the owner of the fields was a distant relative of Naomi's named Boaz. He was impressed with Ruth's hard work and her faithfulness and love for Naomi, so he gave Ruth permission to gather even more grain for herself and Naomi.

Eventually, Boaz fell in love with Ruth and married her. They raised their son together and also continued taking care of Naomi. Ruth ended up with a life more wonderful than she had ever hoped because she made her first priority unselfishly loving and caring for Naomi. When *we* practice unselfish love for others in our lives, we find that it blesses us as well, just as it did with Ruth.

Something to Think About
• Do you let the people you love know that you love them by showing them or telling them?

BIBLE MORALS FOR CHILDREN

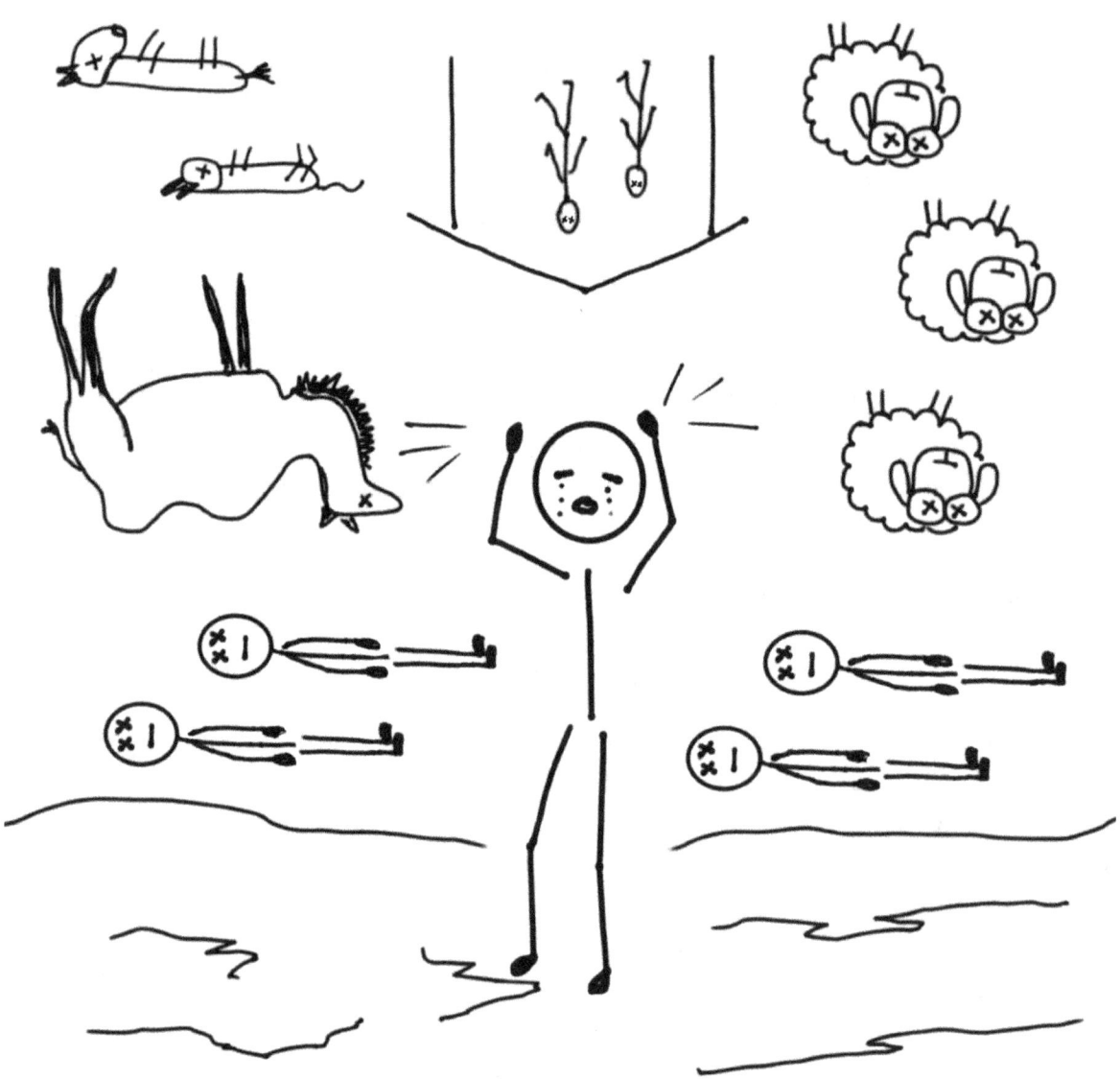

*"The LORD gave, and the LORD hath taken away;
blessed be the name of the LORD."*
(Job 1:21)

Chapter 16

HOW TO DEAL WITH SERIOUSLY BAD DAYS

THE STORY OF JOB

Job 1–42

The story of Job is about a man who truly loved God, but *still* had to deal with some big, serious problems. The Bible says Job was a wealthy man who did good things, obeyed God, and loved his family. One day, God and the devil were having a conversation, and God told the devil what a good man Job was. The devil said anybody would be good if God had given them everything Job had received from God. The devil told God that if Job lost all his blessings, then Job would curse God.

God disagreed. He told the devil he could do anything he wanted to Job except kill him, and Job still would never lose his faith. The devil got to work. In one day, Job received messages that all his cattle, his servants, and his ten children had *all* died, and a strong wind had destroyed his house. To make matters worse, Job suddenly had painful skin sores all over his body! The loss of all he had, along with the physical pain almost destroyed Job, but *still*, he blessed God and refused to blame him.

The next part of the story tells how four of Job's friends talked with him about why these terrible things had happened to him and what he could do about it. Job's friends believed he was being punished by God for some wrong he must have done. They told Job he needed to ask for God's forgiveness. Job disagreed and became angry at his friends because he knew he had lived a good life and God wasn't punishing him. However, Job did wonder why God would let bad things happen to someone good.

Next, God joined the conversation with Job and Job's friends. He told Job that there were many things people don't understand because God is so much greater, wiser, and more powerful than mankind. God told Job to keep his faith and trust in God, and everything would be fine. Job agreed he would follow what

God told him to do. Job's humility and obedience pleased God, so he rewarded him by giving Job *more* of everything he had lost. He was given more property, more animals, and even the birth of new children. Job lived a long, happy life after his difficult experience. "So the LORD blessed the latter end of Job more than his beginning: ..." (Job 42:12).

Job was patient and didn't panic when things in his life went very wrong. He didn't rely on other people's advice about what he should do. He didn't blame God for his problems. Instead, Job turned to God for answers. Job prayed and had faith that God could be trusted to solve any troubles or problems. God blessed Job for his faithfulness!

Something to Think About
• Do you love God only when things are going your way, or do you love him all of the time?

• When bad or discouraging things happen to you, do you get depressed and give up, or do you ask God for help and start working to fix them?

"Thou hast turned for me my mourning into dancing: thou hast put off my sackcloth, and girded me with gladness; To the end that my glory may sing praise to thee, and not be silent. O LORD my God, I will give thanks unto thee for ever."
(Psalms 30:11, 12)

BIBLE MORALS FOR CHILDREN

"And I say unto you, Ask, and it shall be given you; seek, and
ye shall find; knock, and it shall be opened unto you."
(Luke 11:9)

Chapter 17

NEVER, NEVER, EVER GIVE UP!

THE PARABLE OF PERSISTENCE

Luke: 11

Jesus told a parable, an earthly story with a heavenly message, of a man who had a visitor come to his home late one night. He wanted to feed the visitor, but he had no food in his house. He went to his neighbor's house, knocked on the door, and asked him if he could borrow three loaves of bread.

The neighbor called out, "Trouble me not: the door is now shut, and my children are with me in bed; I cannot rise and give thee" (Luke 11:7).

Even though the neighbor refused to give the man any food, the first man didn't return to his house. He remained at his neighbor's house waiting. Jesus said that when the neighbor finally realized the man wasn't going to leave, he got up and gave him the bread. The neighbor gave the bread to the man because he wanted to get rid of the man and return to bed.

Jesus' parable teaches a helpful lesson. When trying to accomplish something in our lives, or when we're praying to God for help with a problem, we sometimes don't find an immediate solution or healing. When that happens, it can be tempting to believe that God doesn't know or care about our situation, and we give up.

But if God knows all things, then he *does* know our needs. If God is all Love, then he *does* care about us. The Bible promises that if we patiently and persistently refuse to doubt God, never losing faith in him, we might not get everything we *want*, but we *will* see that God always provides everything we *need*.

Something to Think About
If you pray and work hard for something and don't get it, do you think it wasn't meant to be and move on? Or, do you think it means you have to work harder and stick with your goal until you accomplish it?

BIBLE MORALS FOR CHILDREN

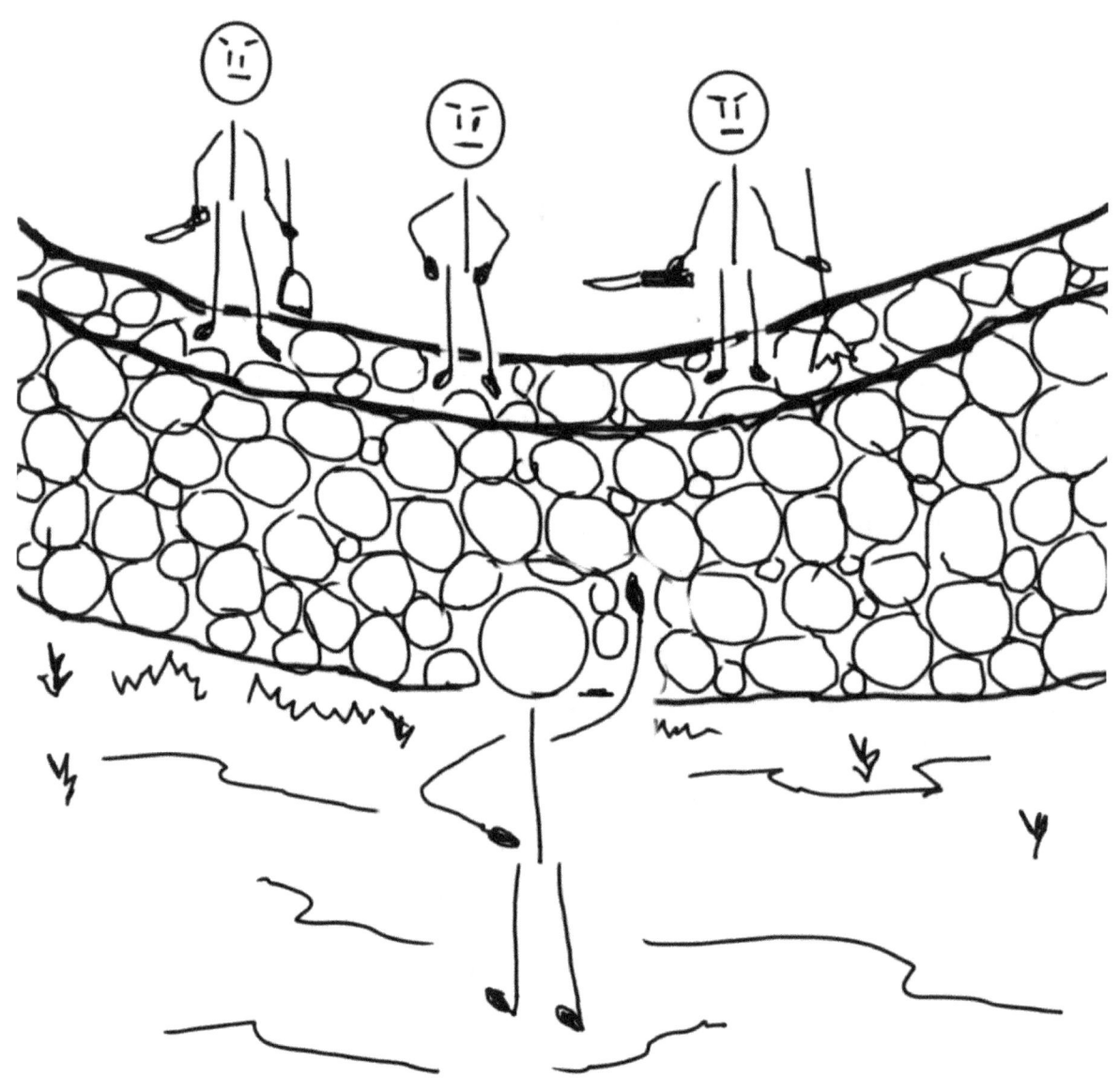

"[L]et us build up the wall of Jerusalem,
that we be no more a reproach."
(Nehemiah 2:17)

NEVER, NEVER, EVER GIVE UP!

NEHEMIAH BUILDING THE WALL

Nehemiah: 1, 2, 4, 5, 6

Nehemiah, a Hebrew, worked for a king in a foreign country. One day, Nehemiah heard that the protective walls around his nearby holy city, Jerusalem, had been destroyed by an enemy army. The city was in ruins, and the people who lived in Jerusalem had given up and hadn't done anything to rebuild the walls.

Having no protective walls around Jerusalem meant the people living there could be attacked again by their enemies at any time. Nehemiah also believed that letting their holy city remain broken down and unprotected was a disgrace to God. Nehemiah felt God was calling him to motivate the people of Jerusalem to rebuild the city's protective walls.

The king Nehemiah worked for gave him permission to leave his job. He traveled to Jerusalem and invited the city residents to hear his plan. They agreed to work with Nehemiah to rebuild the wall, and the work began.

Immediately, three men from neighboring cities who were all enemies of the Hebrews, started doing everything they could to stop Nehemiah's wall-building project. They didn't want Jerusalem and the Hebrews to have a strong, protected city.

First, the three enemies threatened to tell Nehemiah's employer, the king, that Nehemiah was rebuilding Jerusalem so he could take the king's power. This could have turned the king against Nehemiah.

When that threat didn't stop Nehemiah, the three enemies tried to make him give up on building the wall. They told him that his workers could never complete such a big job. Nehemiah ignored their words, kept trusting God, and continued working on the wall.

The three enemies' next plan to stop Nehemiah was to threaten to attack and kill him and his workers. Nehemiah kept praying, told his workers not to be afraid, and passed out weapons to them. He told the workers to hold a weapon in one hand and use the other hand to rebuild the wall.

The last way the three enemies tried to stop Nehemiah was to invite him to meet with them. But the meeting would have delayed finishing the wall project, so Nehemiah told them, "I am doing a great work, so that I cannot come down: why should the work cease, whilst I leave it, and come down to you?" (Nehemiah 6:3).

Just 52 days after the work began, the protective walls around the entire city were finished. Jerusalem was safe! By listening to and obeying God, Nehemiah was protected, and he saved an entire city.

In our lives, whether it's threats to our work or safety, someone telling us we're not talented enough, or being tempted to waste our time, there is nothing that can stop us from accomplishing the good things God directs us to do.

Something to Think About
- What is the best way to deal with people who try to stop you from accomplishing your goals? Ignore them, talk with them, or fight them?

*"Study to shew thyself approved unto God,
a workman that needeth not to be ashamed,
rightly dividing the word of truth."
II Timothy 2:15*

BIBLE MORALS FOR CHILDREN

"And they did all eat, and were filled: and they took
up of the fragments that remained twelve baskets full.
And they that had eaten were about five thousand
men, beside women and children."
(Matthew 14:20–21)

Chapter 18

STOP WORRYING, YOU HAVE ENOUGH

JESUS FEEDS BREAD AND FISH TO THOUSANDS

Matthew 14, 15

Christ Jesus didn't just talk to people about how much God loves and provides for all of us. He proved it. This Bible story tells about two different times when Jesus went into the wilderness with huge groups of people to teach and heal them. At both times, Jesus and the multitude were far away from cities for long periods of time. There was nowhere to buy food, and Jesus' disciples told him he should let the huge crowds go home because they'd be hungry.

Jesus told his disciples not to worry and to start feeding all the people. The disciples told him that there were only a few loaves of bread and a small amount of fish, not nearly enough to feed the more than 4,000 people who were there.

Jesus wasn't worried. He told everyone to sit down and prepare to eat. Next, he took the small amount of fish and bread and gave thanks to God. What was he possibly thanking God for? With all those people and limited food, it would have made more sense for Jesus to beg God to send down more food from heaven!

Jesus knew that whether we see it immediately or not, God is *always* providing for us. If we maintain our faith in this truth, God will help us see that whatever we need is available right here and now. And that's what happened with Jesus.

After thanking God, Jesus told his disciples to start handing out the food to the crowd. "And they did all eat, and were filled: and they took up of the broken meat that was left seven baskets full. And they that did eat were four thousand men, beside women and children" (Matthew 15:37–38).

The food didn't run out, and there was plenty for everyone. There were even many baskets of fish and bread left over!

Someone once said that the most effective prayer is just two words, "Thank you." It's letting God know we're grateful for all our blessings from yesterday and today and confidently trusting him to provide for us tomorrow and forever.

Something to Think About
- How do you feel when you share with others?
- Why do you share with others?
- Do you enjoy sharing, or would you prefer not to share?
- Is there a limit to what you'll share?

"But my God shall supply all your need according to his riches in glory by Christ Jesus."
(Philippians 4:19)

BIBLE MORALS FOR CHILDREN

"Wherefore, if God so clothe the grass of the field, which to day is, and to-morrow is cast into the oven, shall he not much more clothe you, O ye of little faith?"
(Matthew 6:30)

STOP WORRYING, YOU HAVE ENOUGH

BIRDS AND FLOWERS ALWAYS HAVE ENOUGH AND YOU DO TOO!

Matthew 6: 25–34

Wouldn't it be great to never worry again about having enough to meet our needs? The Bible tells us how we can do that. In Jesus' well-known *Sermon on the Mount*, he explained why we shouldn't worry. "Consider the lilies of the field, how they grow; they toil not, neither do they spin: And yet I say unto you, That even Solomon in all his glory was not arrayed like one of these" (Matthew 6:28–29).

Jesus mentioned simple things from nature like flowers and animals, explaining how perfectly cared for they are. He said plants and animals don't plan what they will eat and drink, yet God always provides for them. Jesus said that if God takes such perfect care of these wonderful creations, how much *more* can we trust him to provide for mankind!

Jesus said the important first steps in always having our needs met are to put God *first* in our lives, obey his laws, and follow his teachings. This will keep us thinking and acting in ways that lead to trusting God's unlimited supply of everything we need.

Something to Think About
- Do you spend more time being grateful for what you have, or more time complaining and worrying about what you don't have?
- Which one do you think happy people spend more time on?

BIBLE MORALS FOR CHILDREN

"For thus saith the LORD God of Israel, The barrel of meal shall not waste, neither shall the cruse of oil fail, ..."
(I Kings 17:14)

STOP WORRYING, YOU HAVE ENOUGH

TAKE CARE OF OTHERS FIRST — GOD'S UNLIMITED BLESSINGS

I Kings 17: 8–16

God sent the prophet Elijah to a city called Zarephath in order to help a poor widow and her son. There had been a long drought in that region, and the widow and her son had almost run out of food.

Elijah found the widow in a field and asked her if she would go back to her house to bring him a drink of water. Remember, that was a very big favor to ask because the long drought had made water extremely scarce. The woman recognized Elijah as a prophet of God, so she agreed to get him the water. While she was going, Elijah called to her again and asked if she'd also bring him a piece of bread.

The widow turned to Elijah and said he must not know how terrible her situation was! She only had enough flour and oil to cook one last meal for her son and herself before they starved to death! She explained that she was only in the field to look for two sticks of wood to make her last cooking fire.

Elijah calmly told the woman she could starve if that's what she wanted to do, but wouldn't she please bring him *his* piece of bread *first*? He reminded her of a Bible verse that said God wouldn't let anyone run out of food until it started raining again. "For thus saith the LORD God of Israel, The barrel of meal shall not waste, neither shall the cruse of oil fail, until the day that the LORD sendeth rain upon the earth" (I Kings 17:14).

Elijah's statement must have calmed the woman because she and Elijah returned to her home to do as he had asked. But an unusual thing happened when she went to pour out the last few drops of oil for Elijah's bread. She looked into the oil jar and saw that much more oil remained! When she went to scoop out the last bit of flour for Elijah, she saw that much more flour still remained! Neither her flour nor oil ran out until the drought ended, and she and her son had enough food!

Where was the *miracle* in this story? Was it in some magical property of the flour, the oil, or the containers? Or, was it the wonderful truth that we never suffer for helping others?

Something to Think About

• There are two ways to share with someone. One way is to first give the person what they need, and then you get what's left over. The other way to give, is to first take however much *you* want, and then give *them* whatever is left over. Which way do you usually share?

"Thou openest thine hand, and satisfiest the desire of every living thing."
(Psalm 145:16)

BIBLE MORALS FOR CHILDREN

"[G]o thou to the sea, and cast an hook, and take up the fish that first cometh up; and when thou hast opened his mouth, though shalt find a piece of money: ...."
(Matthew 17:27)

STOP WORRYING, YOU HAVE ENOUGH

YOU OWE MONEY?
JESUS SAYS IT'S TIME TO GO FISHING

Matthew 17

Jesus and his disciples constantly traveled, preaching and healing. There is no record of any of them holding steady jobs or getting paid regularly. One day, Peter, one of Jesus' disciples, was resting outside when a tax collector walked up to him with bad news. Jesus' group owed a tax payment. Peter was worried about how they'd pay it, so he asked Jesus what to do. Jesus knew that God *always* provides for our every need, so Jesus wasn't worried about finding the tax money.

Jesus told Peter how to get the money they needed, but it wasn't what Peter expected to hear. Jesus said, "[Go] thou to the sea, and cast an hook, and take up the fish that first cometh up; and when thou hast opened his mouth, thou shalt find a piece of money: that take, and give unto them for me and thee" (Matthew 17:27).

Peter did as Jesus instructed and caught a fish. When he looked in the fish's mouth, he found the money that was needed to pay the tax!

What is the lesson for *our* lives from this story? Was Jesus telling us that when we have bills to pay, we should look for a fish with money in its mouth? Was Jesus telling us we need to be lucky in finding what we need?

Or, was Jesus reminding us that God is always providing for our needs at every single moment? All we must do when we are in need is to keep living lives in obedience to him, and remember that God supplies what we need. We must be willing to accept what God gives us in whatever way he chooses to supply it. When people have a great need and have no idea how that need will be met, they will often say, "If necessary, it will come out of the fish's mouth." This saying originates from this Bible story.

Something to Think About
- The Bible says that if we trust God and do good, we'll always have something to eat and a place to live. If people lived their lives full of trust in God, do you think they would worry less?

"[T]he LORD appeared to Solomon in a dream ...:
and God said, Ask what I shall give thee."
(I Kings 3:5)

Chapter 19

HAVING GREAT WISDOM

SOLOMON'S WISH AND THE BEST ADVICE EVER GIVEN

The Book of Proverbs

A proverb is a wise saying or good advice that can help us in life. The book of Proverbs contains about 800 proverbs that were collected and studied by King Solomon. Solomon was a smart, successful man for much of his life, partly because he followed the common-sense wisdom in Proverbs. Here are some explanations for a few of the best-known proverbs.

"For the LORD giveth wisdom: out of his mouth cometh knowledge and understanding" (Proverbs 2:6).
The most important education is what you learn about God.

"Withhold not good from them to whom it is due, when it is in the power of thine hand to do it" (Proverbs 3:27)."
Take every opportunity you have to help others.

"Whoso keepeth his mouth and his tongue keepeth his soul from troubles" (Proverbs 21:23).
The best way to stay out of trouble is to be careful what you say.

"Train up a child in the way he should go: and when he is old, he will not depart from it" (Proverbs 22:6).
If parents teach their children Bible values, the children will have better lives when they grow up.

"Iron sharpeneth iron; so a man sharpeneth the countenance of his friend" (Proverbs 27:17).
Associating with people who do good things encourages you to do better things with your own life.

"There is a way which seemeth right unto a man, but the end thereof are the ways of death" (Proverbs 14:12).
Many things that *seem* like good ideas can destroy our lives if we aren't careful.

"A soft answer turneth away wrath: but grievous words stir up anger" (Proverbs 15:1).
Staying calm in arguments resolves them, and getting angry makes things worse.

"For the drunkard and the glutton shall come to poverty: and drowsiness shall clothe a man with rags" (Proverbs 23:21).
You will miss opportunities to have a successful life if you eat or sleep too much or drink alcohol.

If you like these examples, there are hundreds more wise sayings waiting for you in the Book of Proverbs.

Something to Think About
• If you were to write a proverb about something wise you have learned about life, what would it say?

*"Wisdom is the principal thing; therefore get wisdom:
and with all thy getting get understanding."
(Proverbs 4:7)*

BIBLE MORALS FOR CHILDREN

"And the king said, Divide the living child in two, and give half to the one, and half to the other."
(I Kings 3:25)

HAVING GREAT WISDOM

SOLOMON'S WISDOM: WHOSE BABY IS IT?

I Kings: 3

King Solomon was one of the wisest and most powerful kings of Israel. Solomon became king when he was young, just 20 years old. God was pleased with Solomon because he was obedient to God and humble about all the power he had as king.

One night, God spoke to Solomon in a dream. God said that because Solomon was obedient to him and treated his subjects well, he would grant him any wish he wanted! Can you imagine all the things you might wish for? Solomon told God that he had enough blessings for himself, and wanted only one thing. "Give therefore thy servant an understanding heart to judge thy people, that I may discern between good and bad: for who is able to judge this thy so great a people?" (I Kings 3:9). The only thing Solomon asked for was the ability to rule his people wisely.

God was impressed that Solomon didn't ask for more power and money for himself. To reward Solomon, God gave him not wisdom alone, but also unimaginable power, more wealth, and even musical ability. Solomon eventually wrote over 1,000 songs known as the *Songs of Solomon*.

Solomon made many wise decisions. One of his famous decisions was about two women who both had newborn babies. Sadly, one of the mothers rolled over onto her baby while they were sleeping, and her baby died. That mother then stole another woman's living baby while the woman was sleeping. When she awoke, the two women began fighting over the living baby. Finally, they went to Solomon to ask him to decide which woman was the baby's true mother. Both of the women told Solomon, "The baby is mine."

After listening to the women, King Solomon took out his sword. The women asked him what he was going to do with it. Solomon told them he would cut the baby in two pieces and give one-half of the baby to each woman since they couldn't agree on who the true mother was. One woman said that his plan was okay with her. The other woman pleaded, "No! Give the baby to her, and don't harm it!" Right away, Solomon knew who the real mother was. How did he know?

Unfortunately, after many years as the king, Solomon started loving his money, power, and women more than God. He had 700 wives and also started worshipping other gods. God was disappointed and angry at Solomon because God had given him everything, yet Solomon still hadn't remained faithful or good. In the end, several wars tore Solomon's nation of Israel apart, and Solomon died a broken, unhappy man.

The story of Solomon has a simple message. Stay humble and obedient to God and our lives will be blessed. Lose obedience and humility, and it's possible to lose everything.

Something to Think About
- What's the toughest decision you have ever made?
- Do you usually pray about decisions, or try to figure them out by yourself?
- What would you ask God for if he offered to grant you any wish?

"For the LORD giveth wisdom: out of his mouth cometh knowledge and understanding."
(Proverbs 2:6)

BIBLE MORALS FOR CHILDREN

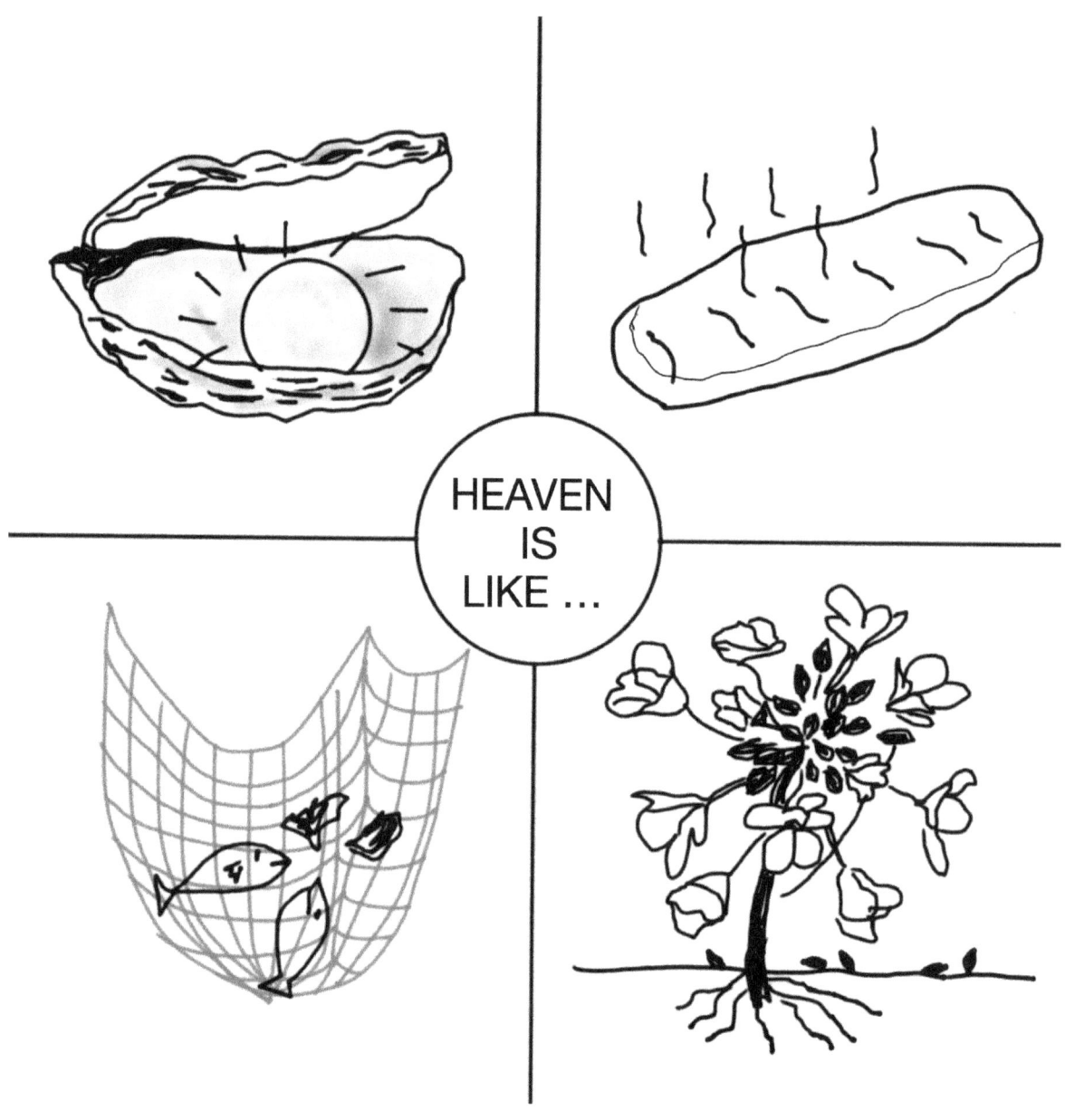

The kingdom of heaven is like ....
(Matthew 13: 31, 33, 45, 47)

Chapter 20

HEAVEN

WHERE IS IT? WHAT IS IT LIKE?

Matthew, Mark, Luke

For thousands of years, people have been fascinated by the idea of *heaven*, a place where people and animals go to be with God after they die.

It's hard to figure out what heaven is like because no one but Jesus Christ ever claimed to have been to heaven and come back to earth to talk about it. Here are some of the things Jesus said about heaven.

Where is Heaven?

Jesus said heaven wasn't far off or up in the sky, but was within us and at hand right here and now. (Luke 17:21) (Mark 1:15)

What is heaven like?

Jesus told many parables to explain what heaven is like and how we can find it in our own lives. Here are a few of them.

Heaven is like fishermen sorting useful things and useless things out of their fishing nets. Our lives become more heavenly when we keep the good things and get rid of the bad. (Matthew 13: 47–48)

Heaven is like the mustard bush, which starts from the smallest seed, but becomes one of the largest plants. Finding heaven in our lives starts with doing small things well. They lead us to opportunities to do greater things. (Matthew 13: 31–32)

Heaven is like a businessman who found the most beautiful pearl in the world, and wanted it so much, he sold everything he had in order to buy it. If we want to have a life of heavenly happiness, we must be willing to make obedience to God the most important thing in our lives. (Matthew 13: 45–46)

Heaven is like a woman making bread who puts yeast into all the dough, so the *entire* loaf will rise. To have a heavenly life, we need to do good things in *all* parts of our lives, not just some of them. (Matthew 13:33)

Heaven is like a group of people who were waiting for a bridegroom to lead them into a wonderful wedding reception. The bridegroom arrived unexpectedly and only half of the people were prepared and able to enter the reception. Those who were unprepared were left outside, and the door was locked. A heavenly life results from being prepared. We don't want to delay living the best possible values and life we can. We risk losing incredible opportunities God provides if we're not ready to act on them. (Matthew 25: 1–13)

Something to Think About
- What is your idea of heaven?
- How do you think you get there? Based on your answer, do you think *you're* going to heaven?

"From that time Jesus began to preach, and to say, Repent: for the kingdom of heaven is at hand."
(Matthew 4:17)

BIBLE MORALS FOR CHILDREN

"God said to the rich man, "Thou fool, this night thy soul shall be required of thee: then whose shall those things be, ...?"
(Luke 12:20)

Chapter 21

MONEY

BE CAREFUL NOT TO FALL IN LOVE!

Luke, Haggai

You often hear people say, "Money is the root of all evil," but that isn't what's in the Bible. It says, "[L]ove of money is the root of all evil: …" (I Timothy 6:10). The Bible contains many stories and examples of how money can *bless* our lives or *ruin* them depending on whether we use money selfishly or unselfishly. Be careful!

Haggai 2:8

"The silver is mine, and the gold is mine, saith the LORD of hosts" (Haggai 2:8). God says that all the silver, gold, and everything, belong to *him*! If that's true, then what we call "ours" or "mine" doesn't belong to us. It's *God's* resources he's letting us borrow. Our lives work better when we remember that everything we have comes from God.

Luke 12: 16–21

Jesus told a parable that showed how people get confused about who truly owns *everything*. He told about a rich man who had so much money and so many possessions that the buildings he stored them in were overflowing. Instead of thinking about how he could share some of his riches with others, the rich man had a different idea.

"And he said, This will I do: I will pull down my barns, and build greater; and there will I bestow all my fruits and my goods. And I will say to my soul, Soul, thou hast much goods laid up for many years; take thine ease, eat, drink, and be merry" (Luke 12:18–19).

The man thought bigger buildings for all of his possessions would make him completely happy! He could relax and think about his riches and how wonderfully he would be able to live.

But God heard the man's plans and told him he was a fool because he would die that same night, and none of his wealth would help him at all. In this story, Jesus taught that life isn't about seeing how much money or how many possessions we can store up for ourselves. Our purpose is to see how many good, kind, and unselfish things we can do for others in our lifetime. These are the things that last, long after we, our money, and our possessions are gone. Our wealth is measured by the good we do for others.

Luke 16: 19–31
Jesus told another story about two men who had died. While on earth, one man was rich and selfishly provided only for himself. The other man, a beggar named Lazarus, was so poor that all he had to eat was leftover scraps from the food rich people threw away.

When both of the men died, Lazarus went to heaven where it was wonderful and everything he needed was there. The rich man didn't go to heaven because of his selfishness and greed. Instead, he went to hell where it was miserable in every way!

In hell, the rich man was suffering and thirsty, so he made a special request to Abraham who was a very important person in heaven. "Father Abraham, have mercy on me, and send Lazarus, that he may dip the tip of his finger in water, and cool my tongue; for I am tormented in this flame" (Luke 16: 24). Abraham refused the request because the rich man had made his choice to be greedy on earth, thinking only of himself, and now he must pay for it in hell. The rich man realized he couldn't make things better for himself, but maybe he could warn his family not to live the greedy, selfish way he had lived on earth. He then asked Abraham if he would at least send Lazarus back to earth to deliver that message to his family.

Once again, Abraham refused the rich man's request and said the rich man's family had the same opportunity as everyone else to listen to his Word and obey God. Abraham added that if God's Word wasn't enough to convince the rich man's family members to change their ways, then *nothing else* would convince them, not even Lazarus himself coming back from the dead.

Luke 21: 1–4
Jesus sat in the temple one day watching people put their offerings to God in a special box where everyone could see how much they gave. Rich people made a big deal out of showing how much money they offered. They wanted others to

see how generous they were, even if it was almost nothing when compared to their great wealth.

Then Jesus saw a poor widow come up to the box. She put in less than half-a-penny, but it was all of her money. She had nothing else! Jesus told the people around him that the widow's offering to God was far greater than the rich men's gifts. They had given just a small part of what they had, but she had sacrificed everything.

Jesus' lesson is that when we do something for someone else, the test of our gift's value isn't about how fancy or expensive it is, but in how much we *sacrifice* when we give.

Something to Think About
- Pastor John Wesley once said, "Whenever I get any money, I get rid of it as quickly as I can, before it has a chance to get into my heart." What was he really saying?
- Has money ever gotten into your heart?

BIBLE MORALS FOR CHILDREN

"How is it that ye sought me? wist ye not that I must be about my Father's business?"
(Luke 2:49)

Chapter 22

BEING SMART

DOES BEING SMART HAVE ANYTHING TO DO WITH GOD?

Luke 2:42–52

When Jesus was 12 years old, he went with his family to Jerusalem to celebrate a Jewish holy day. At some point, Jesus wandered off from his family without telling them. They searched for him all over for three days before they finally found him in the temple, sitting in a group of the smartest religious men of the city, even though he was still a young boy. Jesus wasn't quietly listening as the men talked about God. He was asking them questions about difficult topics boys his age usually knew nothing about.

Other people in the temple, including his parents, were amazed! They wondered how a young boy could be that smart and know so much. Jesus implied that he was using the unlimited intelligence God gives to each of us. The Bible refers to this intelligence as the "mind of Christ" (I Corinthians 2:16).

When children start going to school, many of them are told that there are things too difficult for them to learn or do. They might be told they aren't good at math or that they can't read well. Teachers, counselors, and even parents often believe a child's ability to learn is limited by many different things.

This Bible story gives us a clue how we can be smarter and learn better. Jesus said that the incredible things he did were not miracles. He said that the things he did were things each of us could also accomplish — and even more! "Verily, verily, I say unto you, He that believeth on me, the works that I do shall he do also; and greater works than these shall he do; because I go unto My Father" (John 14:12). The next time we're tempted to believe something is too hard for us to learn, we need to remember that the Bible says, "we have the mind of Christ (I Corinthians 2:16). Our ability to learn is unlimited!

Something to Think About

One way to pray about schoolwork is to beg God to rescue our limited brain and give us the right answers. Another way to pray about learning is to know that God always provides us with whatever we need to know whenever we need to know it.

- Which approach to learning have you tried? How did it work?

"For God giveth to a man that is good in his sight wisdom, and knowledge, and joy: ...."
(Ecclesiastes 2:26)

BIBLE MORALS FOR CHILDREN

"And he fell to the earth, and heard a voice saying unto him, Saul, Saul, why persecutest thou me?"
(Acts 9:4)

Chapter 23

FROM WORST TO BEST IN 3 DAYS

PAUL

Acts

Think of the worst enemy you can imagine, someone who wants to kill you because he hates you so much! Now imagine that just three days later, this person comes up to you and says that God told him he needs to be a good person, so he now wants to be your best friend! I think most of us would believe this person was trying to trick us. We'd probably be afraid of being anywhere near him!

This is how the story started for the Jewish man who finally became known as St. Paul, but who was originally known as Saul. Shortly after Jesus was crucified, Saul spent his time capturing Christians, and taking them to Jerusalem to be killed.

One day, Saul was on his way to a city called Damascus to capture more Christians. Suddenly, he was blinded by a light from the sky and heard a voice telling him to stop hurting Christians. "Saul, Saul, why persecutest thou me?" (Acts 9:4). Saul asked who was talking to him, and the voice said it was Jesus Christ.

Saul asked Jesus what he wanted him to do. Jesus told him to enter a nearby town where he would be told. When the light and voice stopped, Saul was completely blind, so his friends had to lead him to a house in the city. Saul didn't eat or drink anything for three days. He spent all of his time praying to know what God wanted him to do with his life since he would no longer be involved in capturing and killing Christians.

Meanwhile, with Saul still blind, God told a Christian named Ananias to go to Saul and heal his blindness. Saul had such a terrible reputation for getting Christians killed that Ananias asked God if he was sure he wanted Saul to be able to see again. God said he was sure because he had specifically chosen Saul to do many great things with his life. That turned out to be an understatement!

As soon as Ananias healed Saul's blindness, Saul immediately went out among the local people to convince them to become Christians, too. From that time forward, Saul was called Paul.

The local Christians were afraid to work with Paul. Just a few days earlier, he had been trying to capture them and have them killed! Paul finally convinced the Christians that his conversion to Christianity wasn't a trick. He became such a strong Christian that the Jews who used to work with Paul to kill Christians, now wanted Paul killed!

Paul became the most influential follower of Jesus in history and wrote almost half of the books in the Bible's New Testament. These books were originally letters Paul wrote to new communities of Christians. Paul gave them encouragement and guidelines for how the followers of Jesus should act.

After being struck by that light from heaven on the road to Damascus, the rest of Paul's life became one of the most amazing stories in the history of mankind. For many years, he traveled all over his part of the world spreading Christianity, healing, and helping others in the name of God.

The Jews, Romans, and other non-Christians hated Paul for spreading Christianity. He was repeatedly beaten, whipped, stoned, put in prison, and eventually killed for teaching others about God and Jesus Christ. Paul is remembered for teaching others that they should live a godly life and also for the godly life he lived!

Paul's example of how to live a Christian life was simple: follow the example of Jesus' life, love God and others unselfishly, forgive those who try to harm you, and maintain your faith courageously. Paul stood *for* good and *against* evil until the day he was executed by the Romans. It is believed that one of his final statements was, "I have fought a good fight, I have finished my course, I have kept the faith:" (II Tim. 4:7). He certainly did! The life of St. Paul has inspired people for almost two-thousand years and still does today.

Something to Think About
• If you were struck by a divine Light like St. Paul, what do you think God would tell you to immediately change about *your* life?

*"And God wrought special miracles
by the hands of Paul:"*
(Acts 19:11)

BIBLE MORALS FOR CHILDREN

*"Prove thy servants, I beseech thee, ten days; and let them give
us pulse to eat, and water to drink."*
(Daniel 1:12)

Chapter 24

DOES NUTRITION MATTER?

NO!

Daniel 1

Daniel was a boy who was living in Jerusalem when the city was captured by King Nebuchadnezzar. The king wanted to develop a *super group* of young, smart children from among the many different peoples his army had captured. Nebuchadnezzar told his servants to pick a group of the most outstanding young men from Jerusalem and add them to the group. Daniel and three others were chosen, but it wasn't such an honor.

First of all, the King didn't believe in the One God that Daniel and the other three boys worshipped. Secondly, the King decided to give all of the boys new names based on his own country's culture. Third, the boys were required to attend school where they were taught about the King's gods and mythology, things Hebrews didn't believe. David didn't like any of these changes, but he went along with them.

Last, Nebuchadnezzar ordered the four Hebrew boys to eat the same foods and drink the same wine the king ate and drank. The king believed his royal food and rich diet would make the boys bigger, healthier, and smarter than if they continued to eat the plainer foods they usually ate. The king's order was unacceptable to Daniel. The king's meat and wine would have included items that violated the Hebrew's religious laws about food. Also, the king's food had probably been previously offered to the king's gods, so Daniel might have worried that he would also be worshipping those gods or idols if he ate the king's food.

No one forced Daniel to take a stand for his morals, religious beliefs, and values, but he decided to stay true to them. He asked the servant who delivered the food if he and his three friends could instead eat a vegetable mixture called *pulse* and drink water. "Prove thy servants, I beseech thee, ten days; and let them give us pulse to eat, and water to drink (Daniel 1:12).

This request scared the servant. If the boys didn't grow, they would be too weak to learn well in school, and the king would notice the size difference between Daniel's group and the other boys. The king might then kill the boys and the servant, too! Daniel begged the servant to allow his group to eat the pulse and water as a test for ten days to see what the results would be. The servant agreed. Ten days later, Daniel's group was bigger and healthier than the other children who ate the king's meat and drank his wine, and they became ten times smarter than the king's smartest men.

Daniel was willing to compromise on some of the King's demands such as education and name changes, but Daniel refused to compromise his beliefs about worshipping God. He decided to take a stand even if it meant putting his life in danger. What was the result of Daniel's refusal to compromise his religious beliefs and values? King Nebuchadnezzar was so impressed with Daniel's wisdom, he was promoted to important jobs and went on to serve several different kings.

Later in the Bible in Matthew 15:11, Jesus took the lesson about eating a step further. He said people are not harmed by what goes *into* their mouths: meaning what they eat, but by what comes *out* of their mouths in words.

Daniel didn't suffer from eating only the pulse and drinking water. Instead, the wise words and strong principles that came out of Daniel's mouth protected him and gave him a wonderful life.

Something to Think About
• If you were offered anything you wanted in life and all you had to do was change your moral values about what is right and wrong, would you do it?
• What was an experience that tested your commitment to your morals and values?

"It is written, Man shall not live by bread alone, but by every word that proceedeth out of the mouth of God."
(Matthew 4:4)

BIBLE MORALS FOR CHILDREN

"[A]nd he [Moses] looked, and, behold, the bush burned with fire, and the bush was not consumed."
(Exodus 3:2)

Chapter 25

LOOK AGAIN!

MOSES AND THE BURNING BUSH

Exodus: 3

Moses was living in a land outside of Egypt, but he wanted to go back to rescue his Hebrew people from Egyptian slavery. The problem was, Moses had no idea how it could be accomplished.

Tending sheep one day, Moses came across a burning bush, but the bush didn't burn itself up. Instead of walking by, Moses stopped to investigate this strange sight. Suddenly, God started talking to him from out of the bush! God told Moses to go back to Egypt and tell Pharaoh to let the Hebrews go free.

Moses wanted to obey God, but he had a lot of questions about what God was telling him to do. He told God that since the Hebrews didn't yet know the One God, they would ask Moses the name of who sent him to rescue them. "And God said unto Moses, I AM THAT I AM: and he said, Thus shalt thou say unto the children of Israel, I AM hath sent me unto you" (Exodus 3:14). God said to tell the Hebrews his name was I AM, meaning that God is eternal and forever.

Moses' next fear was he wouldn't be able to stand against the power of Pharaoh. God answered that fear by showing Moses how God's power could do anything! God turned Moses' walking stick into a poisonous snake and then back again. He also showed Moses how a serious disease could be healed instantly.

Moses' last fear was he wouldn't be able to talk to Pharaoh because Moses had a speech problem. God comforted Moses by explaining he would tell Moses what to say and would help him say it clearly. God's answers made Moses confident he could return to Egypt and convince Pharaoh to free the Hebrews.

When Moses returned to Egypt, he convinced Pharaoh to let the Hebrew slaves go free, persuaded them to follow him to freedom, and eventually led thousands of the slaves to the Promised Land.

All of these good things happened because Moses was willing to obey God even when the message came from an unexpected source, a burning bush. The job that God gave Moses seemed impossible. By fearlessly listening to God, Moses was able to save the Hebrews. Many other people in the Bible learned this same lesson — nothing is impossible with God!

Something to Think About
- Have you ever asked God to help you with something?
- Has God ever told you to do, or not do, something?
- Think of something you're not good at. If God told you go do it publicly, would you do it?

LOOK AGAIN!

"Therefore the Lord himself shall give you a sign; ...."
(Isaiah 7:14)

BIBLE MORALS FOR CHILDREN

"And the LORD opened the eyes of the young man; and he saw: and, behold, the mountain was full of horses and chariots of fire round about Elisha."
(II Kings 6:17)

LOOK AGAIN!

ELISHA AND THE CHARIOTS OF FIRE

II Kings: 6

The king of Syria was at war with the king of Israel. He had repeatedly tried to capture the king of Israel's army, but every time he went to do it, he found that the Israelite's army had already moved. The king of Syria wondered how this kept happening.

Syria's king got angrier and angrier. He believed that one of his own soldiers was a spy who was helping Israel. The Syrian King's servants told him it wasn't a spy in his own army. They said it was the Hebrew prophet, Elisha, who was helping the king of Israel.

The Syrian king was furious. He decided to send his army out that night to surround the town where the prophet Elisha and his servant were living. When the servant came out of Elisha's building the next morning, he saw that the town was completely surrounded by the Syrian king's army! The servant ran back to Elisha and told him how hopeless the situation looked. Elisha wasn't scared. He prayed to God, asking him to open the eyes of his servant to see how perfectly God was protecting them. The servant went outside again, and this time, he saw something much different. "And the LORD opened the eyes of the young man; and he saw: and, behold, the mountain was full of horses and chariots of fire round about Elisha" (II Kings 6:17). The Syrians entire army was surrounded by horses and chariots of fire to protect Elisha.

At Elisha's request, God struck the entire Syrian army blind, and Elisha led the Syrian soldiers back to Israel. The Syrian captives were afraid they would be destroyed by the Israelites, but the Israelites had mercy on them and allowed them to return to their own country in peace. The Syrians never attacked Israel again. Also, the Syrian soldiers' sight was restored after Elisha asked God to heal them.

The safe and peaceful conclusion of this war came about because Elisha trusted in God's ever-present care and protection even when it seemed hopeless. When Elisha prayed and saw how *God* saw their situation, it changed. Elisha saw that God had *already* provided the protection they needed. When we feel like we are in danger or helpless, we can trust God the same way.

Something to Think About
- When something unexpected scares you, how do you overcome your fear?

LOOK AGAIN!

"The LORD thy God in the midst of thee is mighty; he will save, he will rejoice over thee with joy; he will rest in his love, he will joy over thee with singing."
(Zephaniah 3:17)

"God is no respecter of persons: But in every nation he that feareth him, and worketh righteousness, is accepted with him."
(Acts 10:34–35)

Chapter 26

THE BIBLE AND RACE

WHAT COLOR IS GOD'S SKIN?

Matthew: 6

The Bible talks about people of many different races and countries. It talks about Egyptians, Jews, Greeks, Africans, Romans, Middle Easterners, and more! For centuries, many of these people fought against other races as well as against their own people. Worshipping hundreds of different gods, much of their fighting was about which race or ethnicity was the best and most favored by their gods.

As we read our way through the Bible, we find more and more people believing in the One God. Did they reason that if the One God is everyone's Father, then we all must be brothers and sisters? If so, then it doesn't matter what we look or talk like because God loves all of his children the same. Here are several famous Bible verses speaking to God's love for all of us.

"Have we not all one Father? hath not one God created us …?" (Malachi 2:10).

"God is no respecter of persons: But in every nation he that feareth him, and worketh righteousness, is accepted with him" (Acts 10:34–35).

"There is neither Jew nor Greek, there is neither bond nor free, there is neither male nor female: for ye are all one in Christ Jesus" (Galatians 3:28).

God plays no favorites! It makes no difference who we are or where we are from. God loves us all.

The most famous Bible verse about who God loves the most is a prayer Jesus taught his disciples, his students. They asked Jesus how to pray, and in the first two words, he told his followers why God loves us all equally. "Our Father which art in heaven, …" (Matthew 6:9). Notice Jesus didn't say, Our White, Black, or Brown Father. He said, *Our Father*, meaning God is everyone's Father.

Anyone who has brothers or sisters knows that disagreements and fights sometimes happen, but when it gets out of hand, a good parent always steps in. They often say, "This is your brother or sister, your own family! You need to stop fighting!"

The same is true for all of us today. If we truly share the same Heavenly Father, and we do, then we all are brothers and sisters, the same family. If the world is ever going to stop fighting, then knowing that everyone is our brother — and *treating* them that way — is how the world will finally find peace. Knowing this truth could also bring peace into our individual homes.

Something to Think About
• In one place in the Bible, Jesus is described as *fair*. In another place, he's described as having feet the color of *bronze*. In still another place, Jesus is described as having hair like *wool*. Was he White because he was *fair,* or Latino because his feet were the color of *bronze*? Was he Black because his hair was like *wool*?

• Would it make any difference to you *what* Jesus' race was, or what he looked like?

"Of a truth I perceive that God is no respecter of persons: But in every nation he that feareth him, and worketh righteousness, is accepted with him."
(Acts 10:34, 35)

BIBLE MORALS FOR CHILDREN

"Is it well with the child? And she answered, It is well."
(II Kings 4:26)

Chapter 27

DEATH ... AND LIFE RESTORED!

"IT IS WELL" — THE SHUNAMITE'S SON

II Kings 4

An old woman and her husband lived in a small town called Shunem. The prophet Elisha would often stop by their home on his travels in the region, and they would always give Elisha something to eat as a kindness. One day, the woman suggested to her husband that they build a little room with a small table, a candle, and a bed for Elisha. He would then have his own space to pray or sleep if he wanted a longer rest at their home. Elisha was grateful for the woman's generosity. In return, he wanted to do something to show his gratitude to her. He saw she was quite old and had never been able to have children. Elisha told her she would get pregnant and soon have a child. Not much later, she did have a son, and she loved him dearly.

Some years later, the Shunamite's son became ill when he was working in the fields with his dad. Servants were told to take the boy to his mother in the house, but as she held him, he died in her arms. The woman didn't panic. She placed her son's body on the prophet's bed, and immediately went to see Elisha who had made her son's birth possible.

Elisha, being a prophet, knew what the problem was when he saw the Shunamite woman approaching his home. He sent his servant out to greet the woman and told him to ask her, "Is it well with your son?"

Imagine how the woman might have answered. "Of course it's not well! My son is dead!" Despite the outward appearance of her son, the woman didn't answer that way because she knew in her heart that her son's life was forever in God. Instead, she replied, "It is well" (II Kings 4:26). Elisha heard this statement of the woman's total faith in God and joined her on the trip back to her home. When they arrived, Elisha went into the room where the boy's body lay and shut the door. He lay down on the bed with the boy and prayed, and the boy came back to life. You can imagine how grateful the mother was!

How could the Shunamite woman have said to Elisha that her son was well when to outward appearances he was dead? There would seem to have been no reason for hope. Perhaps it was because the mother believed that the Bible's promise was true, "With men this is impossible; but with God all things are possible" (Matthew 19:26).

Something to Think About
• If you could pray to God to bring someone back to life, who would it be and why?

*"For the law of the Spirit of life in Christ Jesus hath made
me free from the law of sin and death."*
(Romans 8:2)

BIBLE MORALS FOR CHILDREN

*"Then said Martha unto Jesus, Lord, if thou hadst been here,
my brother had not died."*
(John 11:21)

DEATH ... AND LIFE RESTORED!

DEAD OR "JUST SLEEPING?" — LAZARUS, JAIRUS' DAUGHTER

John: 11, Mark: 5

More than any other stories in the Bible, the examples of people who died and were brought back to life are considered the most amazing. Jesus Christ did more of this type of healing than anyone else. Lazarus and Jairus' daughter are two well-known examples of Jesus raising people from the dead.

In the first incident, Jesus wasn't notified that his friend, Lazarus, had died. By the time Jesus got to where Lazarus was, he had been dead for four days and was already buried in a rock tomb.

In the second incident, Jesus was visited by Jairus, an important religious man who had heard of Jesus' healing ability. He came to ask Jesus to heal his 12 year-old daughter who had died that day.

At the homes of both Lazarus and Jairus, Jesus was surrounded by friends and family members who were mourning the people who had died. The friends and family members had no faith that either Lazarus or Jairus' daughter could ever be brought back to life. Jesus calmly told everyone, "Be not afraid, only believe" (Mark 5:36).

But that wasn't easy sometimes, even for Jesus. In Lazarus' situation, Jesus was close friends with his family. When he saw all of them sad and crying, the Bible says Jesus also started crying. It must have been extremely sad when Jesus saw Jairus' little 12 year-old daughter laying there dead and everyone grieving.

With both Lazarus and Jairus' daughter, Jesus didn't say he was going to bring them back to life. Instead, he said an unusual thing no one understood. He said he was going to "awake him out of sleep" (John 11:11). What? Why did Jesus say they were sleeping when it was obvious to everyone else they were dead?

In both situations, Jesus knew that if Life is God as the Bible teaches, then Life is always *here* because God is always here. Jesus' prayers acknowledging eternal Life made both Lazarus and Jairus' daughter respond to the Bible's encouragement. "Awake thou that sleepest, and arise from the dead, and Christ shall give thee light" (Ephesians 5:14).

When Jesus called Jairus' daughter to sit up, she did! In Lazarus' situation, Jesus thanked God for Lazarus' life *before* Lazarus even moved in the tomb. Wow! Can you imagine what it would have been like to see those things happen first-hand?

Jesus' followers were overwhelmed by the healing work he did for people and were in awe of him personally. But Jesus made them still another amazing promise "I say unto you, He that believeth on me, the works that I do shall he do *also* [emphasis added]; and greater works than these shall he do; because I go unto my Father" (John 14:12). Wasn't Jesus saying that the things he accomplished are possible for all of us?

Something to Think About
- Have you ever tried praying about a seemingly hopeless situation?

DEATH ... AND LIFE RESTORED!

Jesus said, "Weep not; she is not dead, but sleepeth."
(Luke 8:52)

BIBLE MORALS FOR CHILDREN

"Speak, LORD; for thy servant heareth."
(I Samuel 3:9)

Chapter 28

ANSWERING GOD'S CALL

"SAMUEL!"

I Samuel 3

What would you do if God called you? What if he called you when you were only 11-years-old? This was the situation that occurred with the prophet Samuel.

Samuel was living and working in a holy temple as an assistant to a priest named Eli who was in charge of the temple. One night when Samuel lay down to sleep, he heard a voice in the dark that called out, "Samuel, Samuel!" Samuel got out of bed and walked into Eli's room. He asked the priest what he wanted, but the priest said he had not called him.

Samuel again lay down in his bed, and again he heard, "Samuel! Samuel!" Samuel went to Eli's room, and Eli repeated to Samuel to return to bed because he had not called him.

Trying to go back to sleep, Samuel heard his name called a third time, "Samuel! Samuel!" Once again, Samuel went back to Eli's room. By this time, Eli realized it was God who was calling Samuel, so he gave Samuel different directions. Eli told him that it was God who was calling him and that if Samuel heard the voice a fourth time, he should say, "Speak LORD; for thy servant heareth ..." (I Samuel 3:9).

God called Samuel for the fourth time. Samuel replied he was listening. God then gave Samuel a very unpleasant message to deliver to Eli, but Samuel obeyed and delivered it. Samuel's faithfulness and courage led him to receive more and more honor and responsibility throughout the rest of his life. He became a prophet and even played a part in selecting David as King of Israel. All of Samuel's success started with his willingness to listen to God's direction, and then obey it!

How do *we* react when we feel God is calling us to do something? Samuel could have ignored God's calling and let his fear stop him from responding. Samuel might not have wanted any more responsibilities. He might have thought he was too young or not smart enough to talk with God, but he didn't let his personal feelings or doubts stop him. Samuel listened to God and obeyed, and it changed his life. We all are called by God to do good things. How we respond to those callings determines the quality of our lives.

Something to Think About
- If God called out to you, what do you think he would say or ask?

"I will hear what God the LORD will speak: for he will speak peace unto his people, ..."
(Psalms 85:8)

BIBLE MORALS FOR CHILDREN

"When the Son of man shall come in his glory, and all the holy angels with him, then shall he sit upon the throne of his glory:"
(Matthew 25:31)
"And he shall set the sheep on his right hand, but the goats on the left."
(Matthew 25:33)

Chapter 29

HOW DOES GOD JUDGE OUR LIVES?

JUDGMENT DAY

Matthew 25 and 7

Do you feel like you're a pretty good person and live a pretty good life? Have you ever wondered if God would agree with you?

How does God decide whether or not we have lived good lives or if we deserve a reward or a punishment? Does God care how much money we have or how well we do in school? Does he care if we're good looking, or talented, or live in a fancy house? Jesus gave a short talk where he explained what's important to God by explaining how our lives are judged every day.

Jesus referred to all of the people in the entire world as belonging to one of two groups. One group, seated on God's right hand, Jesus described as the *sheep*. The other group, the *goats*, is seated on God's left hand. In the Bible, the right side is always the good side.

Jesus said the people on his right hand fed him when he was hungry, gave him water when he was thirsty, befriended him when he was a stranger, cared for him when he was sick, clothed him when he needed clothing, and visited him when he was in prison.

The right-hand people were puzzled because they said they had never seen Jesus in great need. He replied that when they showed compassion to others, it was as if they had shown compassion to him.

Jesus then said to the left-hand people that they did *not* feed, befriend, comfort, clothe, or visit him. The left hand people also said they had never seen Jesus in need. Jesus explained that when they had refused to show compassion to their fellow man in need, it was as if they had refused him.

At the end of Jesus' story, the right-hand people go to heaven, and the left side people go to, uh ... let's just say it doesn't end well for them.

The point Jesus wanted his followers to understand is that our lives are judged moment by moment every day. We're not judged by what we do for ourselves, or by how much we talk or pray about loving God. The value and worth of our lives is found in what we *do* for others.

Something to Think About
- What are some of the things you'd like to improve about the way you live your life?

*"Have mercy upon me, O God,
according to thy lovingkindness: ...."*
(Psalms 51:1)

BIBLE MORALS FOR CHILDREN

*The angel told the woman, "He is not here:
for he is risen, as he said...."
(Matthew 28:6)*

Chapter 30

THE MOST WONDERFUL STORY EVER TOLD

JESUS CHRIST ROSE FROM THE DEAD

Mark 14–16, Luke 24

The story of the life of Jesus of Nazareth, known as the Christ, is often referred to as *the most wonderful story ever told*! Christians believe Jesus was the Messiah or Savior who fulfilled the prophecies of his coming to earth. They believe Jesus was sent to earth by God to save mankind from falling away from God.

In many ways, Jesus appeared to be an ordinary boy when he was growing up. He lived in a small town with his mom and dad and worked with his mom's husband, Joseph, as a carpenter. He grew up with brothers and sisters and worshipped God at the local Jewish temple. but Jesus' short life contained many extraordinary events, including the following.

- He was born of a mother, Mary, who was a virgin.
- Jesus repeatedly healed people through prayer alone of every imaginable problem, including: blindness, deafness, leprosy, physical deformity, mental illness, lack of food and money, and moral issues. Most incredibly, he even brought people back to life who had died, and Jesus taught others how to do those same things!
- He was able to control the weather through prayer alone.
- Jesus could read people's minds and was able to know the past, present, and future.
- Jesus was loving and forgiving when people needed it. He was also strong and tough with people when it was needed.
- Jesus was hated by the Jewish priests even though he did nothing but help people learn about God.
- He was humiliated, tortured, and crucified by the Romans at the request of the Jews, and his body was placed in a tomb. One of the most incredible moments in Jesus' life happened *during* the crucifixion. At the exact time when hateful

people were taking his life, Jesus was praying to God to *forgive* them because they didn't know what a horrible thing they were doing.

• The most wonderful and incredible thing of all is that three days after being crucified and placed in a tomb, Jesus resurrected. He rose from the dead and told his followers there was even more to come! He said he would be with his followers for only a short while because he would leave to be with God in heaven. Several weeks later, Jesus did exactly that! He ascended, or went up from earth to heaven, and his material body disappeared!

More than 2,000 years have passed since those events happened. Billions of people have committed to following Jesus' teachings about God and his personal example. They call themselves Christians, followers of Jesus Christ.

Today, Easter Sunday is the Christian holiday celebrating Jesus' resurrection and his victory over death, the greatest fear all people have.

We all experience the basic principles of crucifixion, resurrection, and ascension in our own lives, in challenges both great and small.

• **Crucifixion**: We must learn to express courage and forgiveness when accused or punished for things we didn't do.
• **Resurrection**: We must learn to not give up when things look hopeless, and to move on with our lives.
• **Ascension**: We must rise to the understanding that nothing can separate us from God and the eternal life we have in him.

Something to Think About
• Why do you think the life of Jesus Christ is called "The Most Wonderful Story Ever Told"?
• Have you ever been accused of, or punished for, something you didn't do? How did you rise above the experience and move on with your life?

*"Jesus Christ the same yesterday,
and to-day, and for ever."
(Hebrews 13:8)*

BIBLE MORALS FOR CHILDREN

"The wolf also shall dwell with the lamb, ..."
(Isaiah 11:6)

Chapter 31

AN EARLY PREDICTION FOR WORLD PEACE

A PROPHECY

Isaiah: 2, 11

One of the most beautiful predictions for world peace ever written is in the book of Isaiah. The prophet stated that this peace would arrive after the long-promised Messiah had come to earth. Isaiah even predicted part of the Messiah's family tree, even though many of those people had not been born when Isaiah wrote it! To Christians, the Messiah and Savior described by Isaiah was — and is — Jesus Christ who was born over 700 years after Isaiah's prophecy!

We hear much about fighting and wars everywhere. It seems impossible that there could come a day when people all over the world would live in peace. Isaiah's prophecy offers Bible readers a wonderful sense of hope, peace, and joy for the future.

"And there shall come forth a rod out of the stem of Jesse, and a Branch shall grow out of his roots: And the spirit of the LORD shall rest upon him, ...;" (Isaiah 11:1–2).

Isaiah was describing Jesus' human family tree. Jesse was an ancestor of Jesus, as were many of the Bible individuals discussed in this book including: Abraham, Isaac, Jacob, King David, King Solomon, and Ruth.

"And it shall come to pass in the last days, that the mountain of the LORD'S house shall be established in the top of the mountains, ... and all nations shall flow unto it" (Isaiah 2:2).

Isaiah predicted the first United Nations-type activity, where all countries would genuinely work together for peace.

"The wolf also shall dwell with the lamb, and the leopard shall lie down with the kid; and the calf and the young lion and the fatling together; and a little child shall lead them" (Isaiah 11:6).

"They shall not hurt nor destroy in all my holy mountain: for the earth shall be full of the knowledge of the LORD, as the waters cover the sea" (Isaiah 11:9).

God was telling Isaiah that in this future world led by the Messiah, even natural born enemies would live in peace: animals just as much as nations.

"And he shall judge among the nations, and shall rebuke many people: and they shall beat their swords into plowshares, and their spears into pruninghooks: nation shall not lift up sword against nation, neither shall they learn war any more. O house of Jacob, come ye, and let us walk in the light of the LORD" *(Isaiah 2:4–5)*.

Isaiah finished this prophecy by saying the Messiah would change everything when he convinced people to obey God. People would stop doing wrong things. They would stop fighting with each other. They would get rid of their weapons and be involved in helping, rather than hurting people. Earth would become more like heaven!

Something to Think About
"If every group of two people could get along, war would be impossible." (*Scott Street*)

• Based on this thought, what is something *you* could do to one of your enemies to help bring peace to the world?

"They shall not hurt nor destroy in all my holy mountain: for the earth shall be full of the knowledge of the LORD, as the waters cover the sea."
(Isaiah 11:9)

BIBLE MORALS FOR CHILDREN

"The Revelation of Jesus Christ, which God gave unto him, ..."
(Revelation 1:1)

CHAPTER 32

THE WORLD'S END AND A NEW BEGINNING

THE BOOK OF REVELATION

Revelation 1-22

A red dragon, a lake of fire, a city of gold, the sun going dark, angels fighting against evil creatures for the future of earth, a special book with seven seals, Satan trying to kill the baby of an unidentified woman, Jesus coming back from heaven for a final Judgment Day, and the world as we know it being replaced by a new heaven and a new earth. All of these stories, predictions, symbols, and more are included in the book of Revelation, the last book in the Bible.

The book of Revelation starts with a *revelation*, something you didn't know before. Jesus revealed information to a man named John, possibly his former disciple or another John in the Bible, about the end of this world and the beginning of a new one.

John was living alone as a prisoner on a barren Greek island called Patmos. John was forced to live there because he refused to stop preaching about Jesus Christ. One day, John heard a voice telling him to write a book containing everything John would be told about the future of the world. When John turned around to see who was speaking to him, he saw a vision of Jesus Christ back from heaven!

Some of the future events John was told about include the following.

• Revelation describes seven new Christian church communities. Two are praised for doing well, and others are warned about losing their faith and the need to be better Christians.

• John receives a vision of what heaven looks like, or maybe John actually went there temporarily and saw it firsthand. He describes a city of pure gold and other beautiful features.

• Revelation includes many messages about secrets to be revealed when the seven seals on a special book are opened.

- God's angels fight against Satan and his angels. God's angels win and destroy the wicked city of Babylon. Satan is thrown out of heaven when he tries to kill the baby of an unknown woman.
- Finally, John describes a new heaven and new earth that will appear, where God and the Lamb, symbolizing Jesus, will live in peace and harmony with all good people forever. Revelation ends with the message from Jesus, "Surely I come quickly" (Revelation 22:20). Jesus says that everything he describes will happen — and soon!

The book of Revelation is a story you'll never forget. Its description of heaven, the final battle between Good and evil, and the end of this world and the beginning of a new and better one is like nothing else. The book of Revelation has challenged, thrilled, inspired, and puzzled artists, scientists, philosophers, teachers, writers, religious and political leaders, and all mankind for over two thousand years. If you're a serious thinker, it will have the same effect on you.

Something to Think About
- What ideas has God revealed to you that give you hope for a new and better *heaven and earth* in the future?

> *"[L]o, I am with you always, even unto the end of the world. Amen."*
> *(Matthew 28:20)*

EPILOGUE

We hope this book encourages you to learn more about the Bible and "The Most Wonderful Story Ever Told."

St. Paul wrote the following words from his firsthand experience.

"The fundamental fact of existence is that this trust in God, this faith, is the firm foundation under everything that makes life worth living...." (MSG, Hebrews 11:1–2).

How do *we* find this trust and faith in God that makes *our* lives worth living? Speaking through the Bible, God offers this simple answer:

"And ye shall seek me, and find me, when ye shall search for me with all your heart" (King James Version, Jeremiah 29:13).

And you will.

www.ingramcontent.com/pod-product-compliance
Lightning Source LLC
Chambersburg PA
CBHW081443070526
44586CB00019B/2213